A Golden SCIENCE Guide

BOTANY

by TAYLOR R. ALEXANDER,
R. WILL BURNETT
and HERBERT S. ZIM

Illustrated by
JEAN ZALLINGER

Under the general editorship of
VERA R. WEBSTER

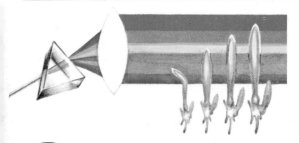

GOLDEN PRESS • NEW YORK
Western Publishing Company, Inc.
Racine, Wisconsin

FOREWORD

Botany is the branch of science that includes every kind of plant life. In combination with Zoology, the study of all animal life, Botany is an essential part of Biology, the study of all life. Due to some basic differences and the fact that so much has been learned about Biology in the last century, it is convenient to separate Botany from Zoology to facilitate learning. However, the reader should never forget that plants and animals, living together, form a complex and unique unity that is the basis for sustaining all life on this planet. This book emphasizes plant science—the diversity of form, the uniformity of processes, the ecological distribution, and the evolutionary development from simple to complex; but, it also endeavors to present the interaction and interdependence of all living forms.

The preparation of any book, and particularly one of this scope, requires the cooperation and assistance of many people. In addition to the co-authors, several people have made outstanding contributions to this one. For this reason, we should like to express our appreciation to George Fichter and to Elizabeth Oliver for their editorial assistance and to Edith Alexander for her assistance to the artist. Art on the following pages was conceived by and rendered in color by Edith Alexander for copying by the artist: 8-9; 10; 13; 14-15; 17; 42-43; 58-59; 68; 101; 103; 104-105; 106-107; 108-109; 112-113; 114-115; 134-135; 141 and 149.

Vera R. Webster
Managing Editor

CONTENTS

Fir

Oak

Orchid

Redwood

Diatoms
(enlarged)

Bacteria
(enlarged and stained)

THE PLANT WORLD

Botany is the scientific study of the many and diverse forms of life belonging to the plant kingdom. Included are trees, shrubs, vines, flowers, grasses, and a multitude of lesser and less-known plants. Botany also treats the structures and functions of plant parts, inheritance, propagation, and interrelationships of plants with each other, with animals, and with their physical environment.

This book, an introduction to botany, deals briefly with plants of the past and their evolution into modern forms. It also summarizes the life histories of the major kinds of living plants, from microscopic bacteria to trees, the largest living things. The book touches also on other major aspects of botany. Here are a few of the many thousands of plant species, illustrating the great diversity of size and form that characterizes the plant kingdom.

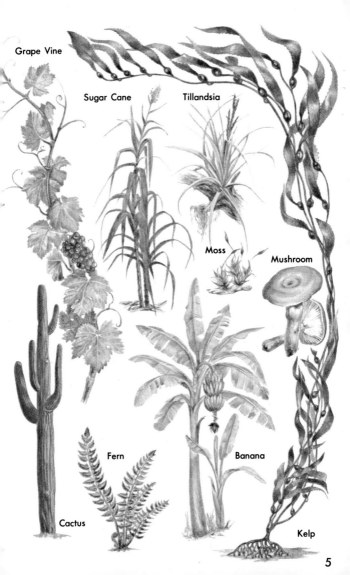

Grape Vine

Sugar Cane

Tillandsia

Moss

Mushroom

Cactus

Fern

Banana

Kelp

5

DISTINGUISHING CHARACTERISTICS OF PLANTS, as opposed to animals, appear both in structure and in response to the environment. The basic living substance of both plants and animals is protoplasm. This complex of living material is usually organized into structural units called cells. Some one-celled organisms have both plant and animal characteristics and are therefore difficult to classify (p. 17). Often these borderline organisms are grouped in a separate kingdom, the Protista; but most plants differ obviously from most animals.

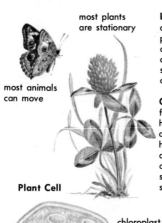

most plants are stationary

most animals can move

LOCOMOTION, a main characteristic of animals, is rare in plants. Most animals can move about freely. Though some plants can move, most grow rooted in soil, or attached to rocks, wood, or other material.

CELL STRUCTURE in plants differs from that in animals. Both have cyctoplasm, a nucleus, and a cell membrane. Plant cells also have a relatively rigid cell wall containing cellulose. Many plant cells contain chlorophylls, essential green pigments found in structures called chloroplasts.

Plant Cell

Animal Cell

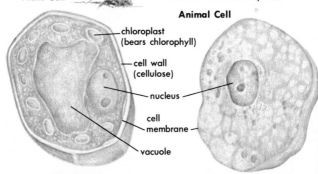

chloroplast (bears chlorophyll)

cell wall (cellulose)

nucleus

cell membrane

vacuole

THE FOOD of green plants is manufactured by the plants themselves. Using energy from sunlight, plants containing chlorophyll combine carbon dioxide and water to form simple sugars. Animals lack chlorophyll and so depend directly or indirectly on plants for food.

GROWTH in typical green plants occurs at the tips of their branches and roots and in the outer layers of their stems; it continues throughout the entire life of the plant. Animals grow in all parts of their body, but growth ceases at maturity.

SPECIALIZED "SYSTEMS" differ in plants and animals but their utilization of matter and energy for life processes is similar. For example, plants produce hormones that have effects similar to hormones produced by animals.

THE LIFE HISTORY of most plants includes two alternating generations. Generation I produces eggs and sperms, and from the fertilized egg of this generation, a Generation II plant develops that reproduces by means of spores. The spores then produce plants of Generation I type. Animals usually have no alternation of generations.

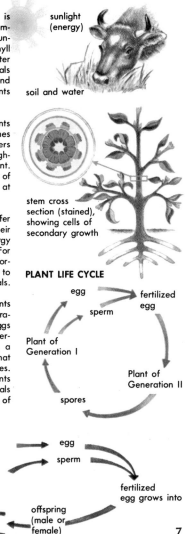

sunlight (energy)

soil and water

stem cross section (stained), showing cells of secondary growth

PLANT LIFE CYCLE

egg → fertilized egg

sperm

Plant of Generation I

Plant of Generation II

spores

ANIMAL LIFE CYCLE

female animal → egg

male animal → sperm

fertilized egg grows into

offspring (male or female)

7

PLANT TISSUES are composed of cells organized to carry on specific functions. Most plant cells are extremely small; an apple leaf, for example, contains an estimated 50 million. Nearly all plant cells follow the same basic plan. They consist of protoplasm with various nonliving inclusions surrounded by a cell wall. Some of the protoplasm is organized into a nucleus that contains inheritance factors and also controls the cell activities. The remainder of the protoplasm is called the cytoplasm. Tissues formed of these cells function for the growth and reproduction of the entire plant. As shown in the diagram, there is a continuity of tissues through the root, stem, and leaf.

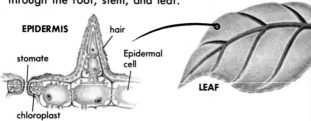

EPIDERMIS — hair — Epidermal cell — stomate — chloroplast — LEAF

MERISTEM TISSUES (growth) consist of rapidly dividing cells that are found in buds, at root tips, and as a thin layer (cambium) between the bark and wood of woody plants. Cambium cells divide to form xylem and phloem tissues.

PARENCHYMA consists of cells that are mainly of one kind. This is the most abundant and the basic tissue of algae and other "lower" plants. Usually it contains thin-walled cells that store or manufacture food. Most of the edible parts of plants consist of parenchyma.

COMPLEX TISSUES are composed of several kinds of cells jointly responsible for a specific function. The mature food-conducting tissue (phloem) has cells with sieve-like end plates through which strands of protoplasm extend from one cell to the next. These serve as passageways for dissolved food. Xylem, another complex tissue, is composed of long, tapered cells and of short, hollow cells that form water-conducting vessels. The epidermis, forming the outer layer of leaves, stems, and roots, also consists of several types of cells, hence is a complex tissue.

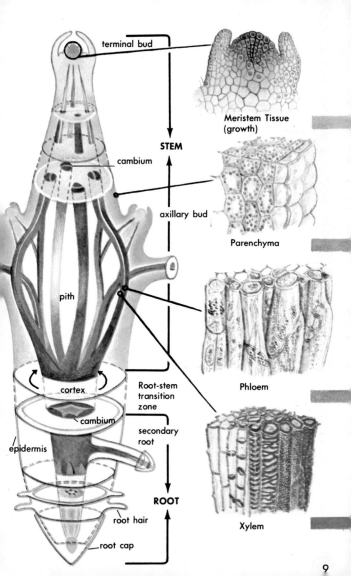

terminal bud

Meristem Tissue
(growth)

STEM

cambium

axillary bud

Parenchyma

pith

Phloem

Root-stem
transition
zone

cortex

cambium

secondary
root

epidermis

ROOT

root hair

root cap

Xylem

9

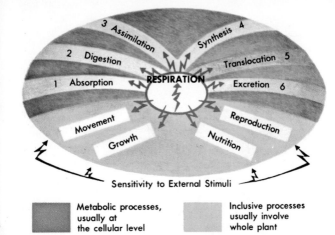

1 Absorption
2 Digestion
3 Assimilation
Synthesis 4
Translocation 5
Excretion 6
RESPIRATION
Movement
Growth
Reproduction
Nutrition

Sensitivity to External Stimuli

Metabolic processes, usually at the cellular level

Inclusive processes usually involve whole plant

BASIC LIFE PROCESSES, such as respiration, growth, reproduction, making or absorbing food (nutrition), and others shown in the diagram above, are essential for the survival of plants. A key process is respiration, which makes energy available to cells and tissues. But because all life processes are interwoven, the malfunctioning of one may seriously hamper the functioning of the others.

METABOLISM is the name for a series of cellular functions that involve the use of energy for life and growth of plants. Respiration involves chemical reactions that release the energy of food for use by cells. Oxygen is usually needed. The energy thus released is used in all processes shown above. The other supporting processes are: (1) absorption, the passage of soluble substances into the cell through the cell membrane; (2) digestion, the breaking down of complex substances for movement in the plant or for use in the cell; (3) assimilation, the forming of new protoplasm from absorbed materials; (4) synthesis, the combining of simple substances to build more complex substances; (5) translocation, the movement of soluble substances through a plant; and (6) excretion, the removal of metabolic wastes. Nutrition is a broad term embracing several processes, especially 2, 3, and 4.

INCLUSIVE METABOLIC PROCESSES

SENSITIVITY is the capacity of protoplasm to respond to such stimuli as light, contact, water, and food. Movement, growth, reproduction, and nutrition in a plant are directly influenced by these external stimuli. A plant's responses to stimuli increase its chances of survival. Responses are adaptations to environment.

NUTRITION is the making and using of food to sustain and repair the living system and to supply the necessary molecules for production of new living material. Green plants produce the foods for all nutrition. These foods must be altered before being used by cells. Most nongreen plants absorb foods from either dead or living organisms. Nutrition is basic to all the other life processes.

MOVEMENT may be by means of whiplike threads in single-celled plants or by redistribution of water among specialized cells in complex plants. Movement of plants is limited, and its occurrence and direction are mainly determined by external stimuli.

REPRODUCTION is the creation of new plants. It maintains a species despite deaths of individuals. The excess supply of variable individuals makes evolution possible. Temperature and length of daylight influence the timing and mechanics of plant reproduction.

GROWTH results from an increase in the number of cells, their enlargement and maturation according to patterns determined by heredity and made possible by metabolism. The direction of growth is determined by such stimuli as light and gravity.

Plant stem grows toward light source and away from gravity.

Motile microscopic algae are dispersed in the water in diffuse light. In a concentrated beam, they aggregate.

When potted plant is turned on its side, the young tissue responds by a change in growth direction.

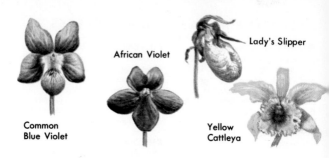

Common
Blue Violet

African Violet

Lady's Slipper

Yellow
Cattleya

THE VARIETY OF PLANT LIFE is tremendous, a result of evolutionary changes that began over two billion years ago. More than 350,000 kinds of living plants are known. Each has been given a scientific name of two parts. The first is the genus; the second is the species. Both words are latinized. A tree called Australian Pine in Florida, Beefwood in California, and Sheoak in Australia, where it is native, is known to botanists in all these places by its scientific name, *Casuarina equisetifolia*. Obviously, some plants have several local names, but each has only one scientific name, which is recognized the world over.

This orderly system of naming and classifying plants was originated in 1753 by the Swedish naturalist, Linnaeus. Used also by zoologists in naming animals, this binomial (two names) system is based on natural relationships as revealed by the study of fossils and also by anatomical and structural similarities. The two purple flowers above are from plants that are not related, though the flowers are much alike in color and general shape and their common names imply relationship. The pink and yellow flowers at the right are closely related, as a detailed study of the reproductive structures in the flowers will reveal. Both are orchids despite different common names.

THE BASIC CLASSIFICATION UNIT is the species. The many millions of individuals of each species may vary somewhat in size, color, and even shape. Some of these differences are consistent enough so that a species may be divided into varieties, but all the varieties can interbreed—a characteristic of a species. With few exceptions, members of different species cannot interbreed. Groups of similar species are combined to form the next category, the genus. Similar genera are grouped in families. Each successively larger category—order, class, division, and subkingdom—contains a larger number of plants. The largest category is the plant kingdom. All living things with cellular structure belong either in the plant or animal kingdom.

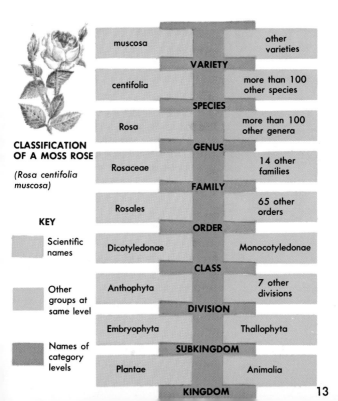

CLASSIFICATION OF A MOSS ROSE

(Rosa centifolia muscosa)

KEY

Scientific names

Other groups at same level

Names of category levels

muscosa		other varieties
VARIETY		
centifolia		more than 100 other species
SPECIES		
Rosa		more than 100 other genera
GENUS		
Rosaceae		14 other families
FAMILY		
Rosales		65 other orders
ORDER		
Dicotyledonae		Monocotyledonae
CLASS		
Anthophyta		7 other divisions
DIVISION		
Embryophyta		Thallophyta
SUBKINGDOM		
Plantae		Animalia
KINGDOM		

THE PLANT KINGDOM pictured as a family tree shows probable relationships of major groups of plants and their development from the more primitive groups at the base. Many plant groups have only scientific names. All are treated in more detail elsewhere in this book. Thallophytes (pp. 16–41), such as bacteria, fungi, and algae, are simple plants. Embryophytes, or higher plants (pp. 42–69), form embryos and, except for the Bryophytes, all contain vascular or conducting tissues.

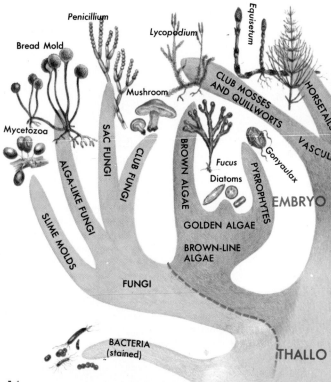

Penicillium

Bread Mold

Lycopodium

Equisetum

Mushroom

CLUB MOSSES AND QUILLWORTS

HORSETAILS

Mycetozoa

SAC FUNGI

CLUB FUNGI

BROWN ALGAE

Fucus

Diatoms

Gonyaulax

VASCULA

PYROPHYTES

EMBRYO

ALGA-LIKE FUNGI

SLIME MOLDS

GOLDEN ALGAE

BROWN-LINE ALGAE

FUNGI

BACTERIA
(stained)

THALLO

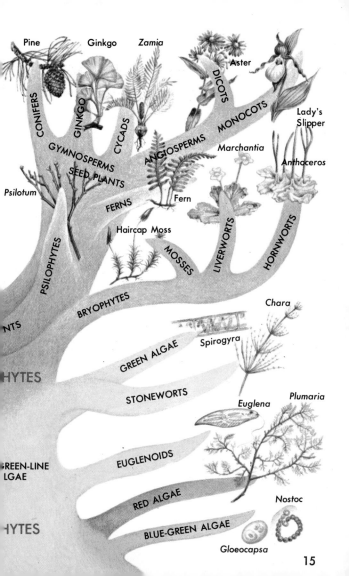

Pine

Ginkgo

Zamia

Aster

DICOTS

MONOCOTS

Lady's
Slipper

CONIFERS

GINKGO

CYCADS

ANGIOSPERMS

Marchantia

Anthoceros

GYMNOSPERMS

SEED PLANTS

Psilotum

FERNS

Fern

LIVERWORTS

HORNWORTS

PSILOPHYTES

Haircap Moss

MOSSES

NTS

BRYOPHYTES

Chara

HYTES

GREEN ALGAE

Spirogyra

STONEWORTS

Plumaria

Euglena

REEN-LINE
LGAE

EUGLENOIDS

RED ALGAE

Nostoc

HYTES

BLUE-GREEN ALGAE

Gloeocapsa

15

Algae, bacteria, and fungi (simple plants that lack roots, stems, and leaves) form the subkingdom Thallophyta. These thallus plants are classified into various divisions based upon types of structures, nutrition, reproduction, pigmentation, and the chemical composition of both cell walls and stored food. Color alone is not reliable for classification. For example, the red-colored alga that gives the Red Sea its name is structurally a blue-green alga. Photosynthesis, the manufacturing of food by using solar energy, occurs in most algae, in only a few bacteria, and in no fungi.

THE ORIGIN OF LIFE is still a mystery. The primitive earth, about 3 billion years ago, was not like it is today. The earth's surface and atmosphere were such that life as we know it today could not have existed.

Earth Without Life (Abiotic)

The first plants helped change this hostile environment and prepared the earth for new forms of life. They helped decrease carbon dioxide and increase oxygen and ozone. Ultraviolet ray penetration was lessened, too, by the new atmosphere.

A POSSIBLE PATTERN of life's origin and change from the beginning to modern times is shown at left. Evidence of the earliest forms of life indicate that they were much like modern bacteria and blue-green algae. They form a group called primitive protista that lack organized nuclei. Slowly other forms evolved from them, first with nuclei but no tissue systems. Some became animal-like, the protozoa. Others became the algae. Fungi represent an intermediate terminal line. The development of tissue systems led to today's higher plants and animals that are highly coordinated organisms.

THE EUGLENOIDS pictured below are three organisms that botanists consider to be plants, but which many zoologists classify as animals. *Euglena* contains chlorophyll and can manufacture its own food. It moves by means of a whiplike flagellum, has a pliable outer membrane but no cell wall, and takes in food and eliminates wastes through its gullet. *Astasia* resembles *Euglena* but lacks chlorophyll, hence is even more animal-like. *Colacium,* in contrast, is more plantlike. It does not move, except in its zoospore (reproductive cell) stage. It contains chlorophyll in distinct bodies (chloroplasts) and has a firm gelatinous cell wall.

The majority of euglenoids, *Euglena*-like plants, are found in organically rich fresh or salt waters. Other euglenoids are parasitic within animals. Totally there are about 500 species.

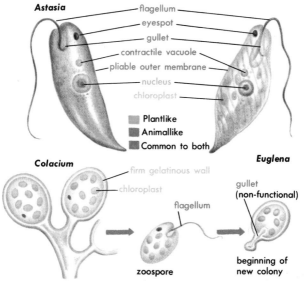

Astasia

flagellum
eyespot
gullet
contractile vacuole
pliable outer membrane
nucleus
chloroplast

■ Plantlike
■ Animallike
■ Common to both

Colacium

firm gelatinous wall
chloroplast

flagellum

zoospore

Euglena

gullet
(non-functional)

beginning of
new colony

17

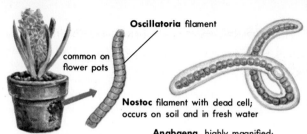

Oscillatoria filament

common on flower pots

Nostoc filament with dead cell; occurs on soil and in fresh water

Gloeocapsa, cells in gelatinous sheath; found on damp rocks

Anabaena, highly magnified; resembles *Nostoc*

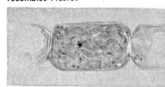

ALGAE

BLUE–GREEN ALGAE, about 1,400 species, are commonly blue-green, but red, violet, yellow, brown, and black species also occur. Extremely simple plants, all are microscopic and consist of a single cell with no well-organized nucleus. The chlorophyll occurs in membranous chloroplast equivalents rather than in distinct chloroplasts. Many live as single cells, others in colonies, or in filaments. They reproduce primarily by simple cell division (fission) or by a fragmentation or breaking up of the colony or filament, each part continuing growth independently. Blue-green algae live in fresh or salt water, in hot springs, on moist soil or other damp surfaces, and as parasites. Some kinds increase soil fertility by producing nitrogen compounds. Others are important as food for young fish and other small water animals. Some species cause the water in swimming pools to be slimy or give reservoirs of drinking water a foul odor and taste. A few kinds are toxic and may cause the death of animals that drink water in which these algae grow.

RED ALGAE are believed to share a common ancestor with blue-green algae. Mainly marine, they grow from tidal shallows to depths greater (600 ft.) than any other plants that manufacture food. Special pigments that trap the feeble light in the deep sea enable the plants to carry on photosynthesis. Red algae are usually small, only a few growing longer than 2 or 3 feet. They are attached to the bottom by holdfasts. Most of the 3,500 species are red or pink, but a few are purple, green, or brown.

Red algae are usually multicellular, each cell with a well-organized nucleus. Most species reproduce sexually. The male sex cells are carried to the female by water currents.

IRISH MOSS (*Chondrus crispus*) is made into puddings. Products of other species are added to ice cream mixes as an emulsifier.

CORALLINA and related species of warm seas secrete lime and help build coral reefs; have been active reef builders in the geo-logic past as well as in recent and present times.

GELIDIUM and related forms produce gelatinous agar, used for solidifying desserts and in culture media for growing bacteria, fungi, and orchids; also used as a filler in commercial foods.

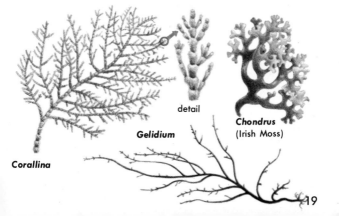

detail

Gelidium

Chondrus
(Irish Moss)

Corallina

BROWN ALGAE contain chlorophylls as other algae do, but they are masked by brown pigments. All brown algae are multicellular, but some are microscopic. The cellulose cell walls are covered by a gelatinous layer of algin. Food is commonly stored as laminarin, a carbohydrate, and mannitol, an alcohol.

Most of the 1,500 species of brown algae are marine. They float freely, or may grow attached to the bottom in intertidal zones or in deeper waters. The Sargasso Sea, an area of eddying seas covering up to 2 million square miles in the mid-Atlantic, contains floating beds of *Sargassum*. Tales of ships being trapped in these masses of seaweeds are mythical, but captains of sailing vessels feared the Sargasso Sea because of its dead calms.

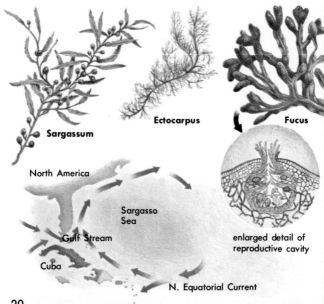

Sargassum

Ectocarpus

Fucus

North America

Sargasso
Sea

Gulf Stream

Cuba

enlarged detail of
reproductive cavity

N. Equatorial Current

Brown algae vary in methods of reproduction. *Ectocarpus* produces both sexual and asexual plants, as do the giant kelps in which the sexual stage is microscopic. *Sargassum* and *Fucus* (Rock Weed or Bladder Wrack) also have an extremely reduced sexual stage. Brown algae are important as food, for fertilizer, and for the production of algin, a food additive.

KELPS (several of which are shown below) are large brown algae that range in length from one foot to more than 100 feet. The plant consists of a holdfast, a long stemlike stipe, and a flattened blade, which may be single or divided. Some of the larger kelps are kept afloat by air bladders. *Macrocystis,* for example, may be anchored 50 feet below the surface; it spreads in floating mats above. Ribbon Kelp *(Nereocystis)*, Laminaria, and the Sea Palm *(Postelsia)* are other common kelps.

COMMON PACIFIC KELPS

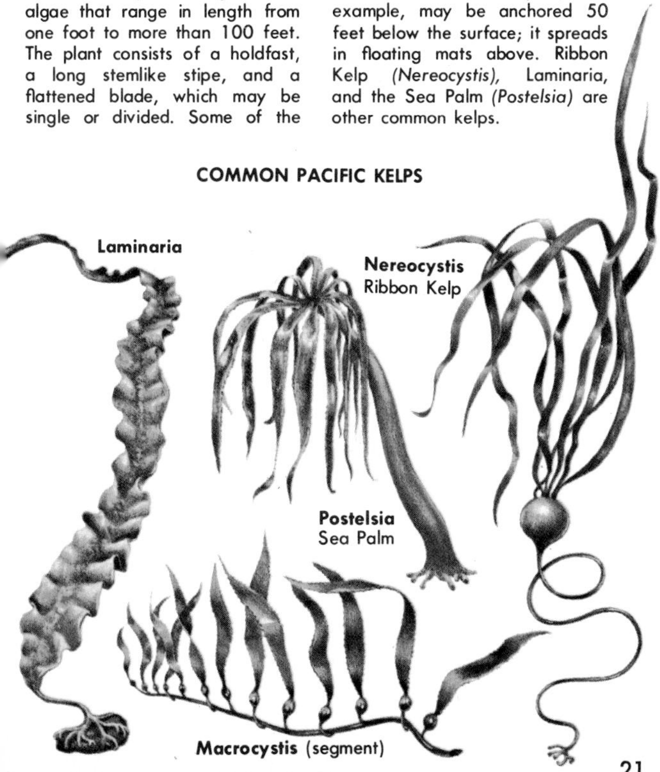

Laminaria

Nereocystis
Ribbon Kelp

Postelsia
Sea Palm

Macrocystis (segment)

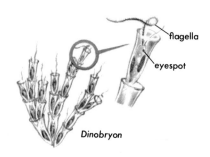

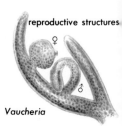

flagella

eyespot

reproductive structures

Dinobryon

Vaucheria

TWO FRESH-WATER GOLDEN ALGAE

GOLDEN ALGAE occur as single cells, in filaments or in colonies. They are mostly yellowish-green to golden-brown, but in some, these colors are masked by bright orange and red pigments. Many are equipped with two flagella of unequal length, as in *Dinobryon*. One of the most common, *Vaucheria*, was until recently classified as a green alga, but like all golden algae, *Vaucheria* stores its food as oils rather than as starch, as do the green algae and most other plants.

DIATOMS (shown on top page 23) are among the most important of the more than 10,000 species of golden algae. Abundant in both fresh and salt water, they are the major constituent of phytoplankton, the floating plant life that is the basic food of nearly all aquatic animals.

All diatoms are microscopic. Each is enclosed in a cell wall of two halves that fit together like a box and its lid. The layer of glass-like silica deposited on the cell wall forms sculptured designs. Kinds and numbers of diatoms found in water can be used as a pollution index.

Diatoms may reproduce either asexually by cell division or by a sexual process that leads to a special type of spore called an auxospore.

Diatom shells are found in layers hundreds of feet thick on lands formerly covered by shallow seas. They are mined as "diatomaceous earth" for use as an abrasive, for insulation, and for filters in various industrial processes. Crude oil deposits possibly originated from the stored oils of diatoms. At extremely high temperatures (above 1000° F) diatomaceous earth is a more effective insulator than asbestos.

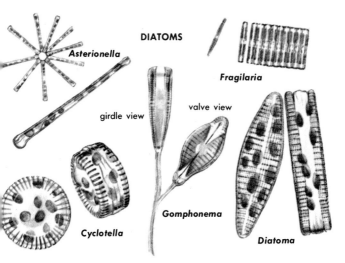

DIATOMS

Asterionella

Fragilaria

girdle view

valve view

Cyclotella

Gomphonema

Diatoma

DINOFLAGELLATES are closely related to the golden algae. Most of the 1,000 species of dinoflagellates have grooved cellulose walls that may resemble plates of armor. *Gymnodinium brevis* is one of several dino-flagellates causing "red tides" that destroy fish and other sea life. Oysters and clams become poisonous after feeding on species of *Gonyaulax* that are most prevalent in the "R-less" months. Luminescent dinoflagel-lates, such as *Noctiluca,* are the most common cause of phosphorescence in the sea. *Ceratium* is a common dino-flagellate in fresh-water lakes.

DINOFLAGELLATES

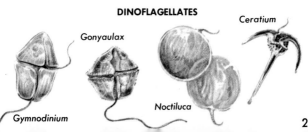

Ceratium

Gonyaulax

Gymnodinium

Noctiluca

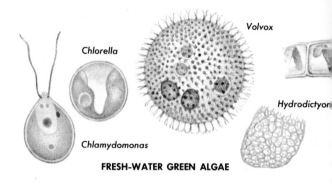

FRESH-WATER GREEN ALGAE

GREEN ALGAE, a highly diverse group of more than 5,000 species, are most abundant in fresh water, where they are food of aquatic animals. They may also grow on moist surfaces, even on such unusual places as turtles' backs and sloths' hair. Some green algae are microscopic, unattached single cells, as *Chlamydomonas* and *Chlorella* (above). Others, such as *Volvox* and *Hydrodictyon*, are small colonial forms. Those with flagella can move independently. The filamentous *Spirogyra* and the desmids have oddly shaped chloroplasts.

Like higher plants, most green algae are green due to chlorophylls. Cell walls containing cellulose and the storage of food as starch are other features suggesting that green algae are the main line of evolution that terminated in seed plants. Yellow to orange pigments, also typical, may mask the green in some green algae. Species of *Chlamydomonas* are often responsible for the appearance of a red coloration in long-standing snowbanks.

Some green algae reproduce both asexually and sexually; some are wholly asexual; others have only sexual reproduction. In some kinds, the life cycle includes two different plant forms.

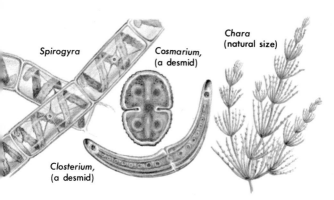

Spirogyra

Cosmarium,
(a desmid)

Chara
(natural size)

Closterium,
(a desmid)

MARINE GREEN ALGAE (shown below) comprise only about 10 percent of the green algae, and many of these are large. Sea Lettuce *(Ulva)* is common along ocean shores, washed in by the tide. *Caulerpa* lacks cross walls in its protoplasm, so the protoplasm, containing many nuclei, extends throughout the plant. *Halimeda* and *Acetabularia* are other attached forms of tropical seas.

STONEWORTS, represented here by *Chara* (shown above), occur in fresh or brackish quiet waters. They differ from all other forms of algae in having their eggs and sperms surrounded by jackets of sterile cells. Stoneworts, about 200 species, are placed in a separate division by some botanists, with green algae by others. *Chara* sometimes becomes a serious weed in fish hatcheries.

MARINE GREEN ALGAE

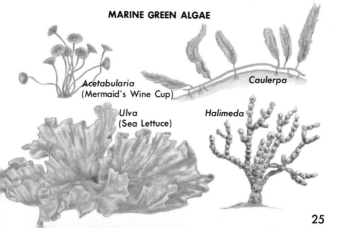

Acetabularia
(Mermaid's Wine Cup)

Caulerpa

Ulva
(Sea Lettuce)

Halimeda

Earth's surface is about three quarters water

Relative Food Production (estimated)

land plants

algae

CULTIVATION OF ALGAE is being considered and experiments are underway to make use of algae as a direct source of food for a growing world population. Algae are ideal food plants. They contain little cellulose. Land crops, in contrast, produce cellulose, a substance that is unusable as food by man and only indirectly by livestock. Under controlled conditions, algae grow the year around; furthermore, they are almost free of pests. At present, man's use of algae is chiefly indirect—through the eating of fish and other sea foods.

Chlorella, a green alga (p. 24) rich in foods and vitamins, is the most used in current experiments. Under suitable conditions, *Chlorella* reproduces very rapidly. By changing its environment slightly in different ways, *Chlorella* can be made to produce from 7 to 88 percent protein, from 6 to 40 percent carbohydrates, and from 1 to 75 percent fats. If *Chlorella* were a crop, an acre useless for ordinary farming could produce 50 tons of foods per year. Even land crops in good soils yield only 5 to 10 tons of dry weight food per year. Though only experimental now, *Chlorella* farming may some day supplement our food supply. Perhaps even sooner it will supply food and oxygen for space travelers, especially if a long voyage to Mars or beyond is undertaken.

Algae—*Chlorella* in particular—are used also in sewage purification. Rapid growth of the algae in treatment tanks releases large amounts of oxygen that is utilized by bacteria in oxidizing the wastes before they are released into streams, lakes, or other waters.

A SPACE STATION, of necessity, must be a closed ecosystem in which materials are recycled to sustain life. A space-unit food factory will work theoretically as shown in the diagram below. In the manufacturing of food, algae can utilize human wastes (processed by bacteria) plus the carbon dioxide and water given off in respiration both by bacteria and man. A by-product of photosynthesis is oxygen, needed by man and the bacteria for their survival. A similar system might be used in submarines, with light being provided by electricity rather than the sun.

Photosynthesis is the basic dynamic process of life and most of the photosynthesis on the earth is performed by algae. For this reason, algae seem best suited as the photosynthetic key to recycling materials and energy in an artificial environment.

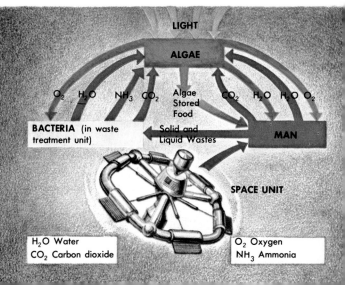

LIGHT

ALGAE

O_2 H_2O NH_3 CO_2 Algae Stored Food CO_2 H_2O H_2O O_2

BACTERIA (in waste treatment unit)

Solid and Liquid Wastes

MAN

SPACE UNIT

H_2O Water
CO_2 Carbon dioxide

O_2 Oxygen
NH_3 Ammonia

BACTERIA

Bacteria are primitive plants that are similar to the simplest blue-green algae and also to fungi. Like some algae, they do not have an organized nucleus. Most are single cells, but some form filaments or masses. All of the 1,700 species are classified by three basic shapes (p. 29) and are microscopic, the smallest only 1/650,000 inch in diameter. Some bacteria require free oxygen; others can live without oxygen.

Some bacteria are parasites; others are saprophytic. Chemosynthetic bacteria get energy by oxidizing iron, sulfur, or nitrogen compounds. A few kinds are photosynthetic; they contain green or purple light-absorbing pigments and get their energy from light. They do not give off oxygen as do other photosynthetic plants.

Bacteria usually reproduce by simple division (fission). Fission may occur every 20 minutes, and the descendants of one bacterium could number 4,700,000,000,000,-000,000,000 in a span of 24 hours. Many produce spores that can survive extremes of heat and cold.

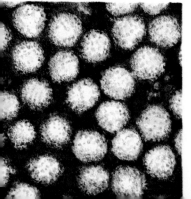

OTHER MICROSCOPIC FORMS, smaller than bacteria, are viruses and rickettsias. Viruses are non-cellular and are small enough to pass through filters that stop bacteria. Polio, rabies, and common colds are virus diseases. Rickettsia, halfway in size between bacteria and viruses, have a cell wall, reproduce by fission, and can also pass through filters. Like viruses, they can be grown only on living media. Typhus is a rickettsial disease.

Rice dwarf virus as seen with electron microscope

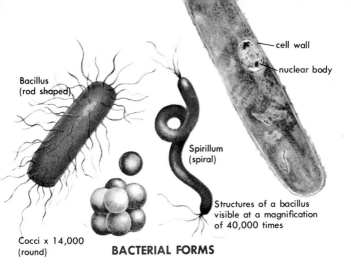

Bacillus
(rod shaped)

Spirillum
(spiral)

cell wall

nuclear body

Structures of a bacillus
visible at a magnification
of 40,000 times

Cocci x 14,000
(round)

BACTERIAL FORMS

USEFUL BACTERIA include many important kinds including those that cause decay. Decay bacteria break down the complex molecules locked in dead plants and animals and change them into simpler molecules that are usable by other plants. Carbohydrates are reduced to carbon dioxide and water; proteins yield nitrogen in the form of nitrates. These chemicals released from dead plants and animals by decay bacteria are thus made available for use again and again. Without these bacteria, all living things, except sulfur bacteria and related forms, would eventually become extinct, for carbon and nitrogen in available forms occur only in limited amounts.

Bacteria are also useful in the commercial production of vinegar, cheeses, acetone, and alcohols.

Many plants and animals are lifetime hosts for great numbers of bacteria, some of which may be beneficial. Clover, alfalfa, and other plants of the legume family have roots with nodules that contain bacteria. These bacteria change nitrogen from the air into nitrates.

29

FOOD SPOILAGE is due mainly to bacteria. In suitable temperature surroundings and with sufficient food and water, bacteria multiply rapidly; and since ancient times, man has used a variety of methods to prevent or to slow their growth so that food can be preserved.

An early method of food preservation still used today is drying. This deprives the bacteria of the moisture needed for growth. Preservatives, such as salt, prevent bacteria from absorbing water. Often the two methods are combined, as in salt-curing and smoking.

Food-spoilage bacteria can be killed at a high temperature—boiling or above. Milk is pasteurized by heating it only high enough to kill disease-causing bacteria. Foods are also frozen or kept under refrigeration to retard bacterial growth. Below-freezing temperatures not only stop the growth of bacteria but also eliminate the water they need.

COUNTING BACTERIA directly is impossible because they are usually so abundant; counting is generally done indirectly by making a dilution series, as shown below.

A measured amount of milk, or other liquid to be tested, is withdrawn and diluted with sterile water. This is repeated, and then the same amount is withdrawn from each dilution and used to inoculate the sterile agar plates. Each bacterium starts a colony on the plate. When only a few colonies are present, which will occur in a large dilution, the counting then becomes easy. The procedure is illustrated below.

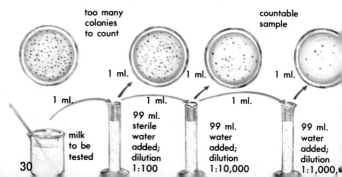

too many colonies to count

countable sample

1 ml.   1 ml.   1 ml.   1 ml.

1 ml.   1 ml.   1 ml.

milk to be tested

99 ml. sterile water added; dilution 1:100

99 ml. water added; dilution 1:10,000

99 ml. water added; dilution 1:1,000,

Bacteria of all three shapes (round, rod, and spiral) cause infectious diseases of man. ▶

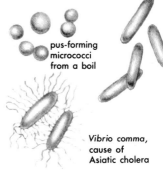

pus-forming micrococci from a boil

Vibrio comma, cause of Asiatic cholera

HUMAN DISEASES caused by bacteria are transmitted (1) through food (botulism, undulant fever); (2) by inhaling respiratory secretions (scarlet fever, pneumonia, tuberculosis, whooping cough); (3) by intimate contact (anthrax, venereal infections); and (4) by insects or other animals (bubonic plague).

PATHOGENIC BACTERIA, those that cause diseases, produce a toxin that poisons the host. Endotoxins are a part of the bacterial cell and are released only when the cell dies. Exotoxins, which are much more potent, are secreted around the cells. Bacteria may be so specialized that they infect only one or a closely related host. Disease bacteria cause many diseases of plants, man, and other animals but the damage they do through disease and decay is far outweighed by their value in the nitrogen cycle and as intestinal symbionts. Some soil bacteria have proved to be a source of antibiotics, which are useful against bacterial invasions.

BACTERIAL PLANT DISEASES are all caused by rod-shaped bacilli. Some cause plant tissues to become "spotted" as the cells around the infection die. Blights and rots are also caused by bacteria. Others cause wilt, by a mechanical blocking of the xylem so that water does not move up freely from the roots. Still others cause galls or other abnormal growths.

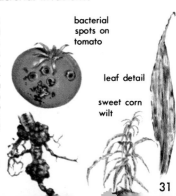

bacterial spots on tomato

leaf detail

sweet corn wilt

crown gall on almond tree root

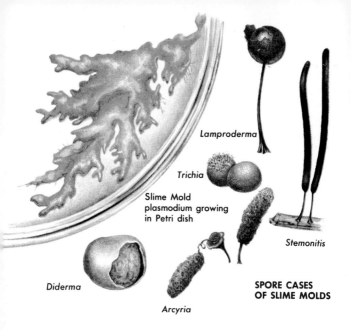

Lamproderma

Trichia

Slime Mold
plasmodium growing
in Petri dish

Stemonitis

Diderma

SPORE CASES
OF SLIME MOLDS

Arcyria

FUNGI

SLIME MOLDS (Myxomycophyta) are fungus-like plants that, lacking chlorophyll, are either saprophytic or parasitic. Totaling about 500 species, these molds are well named, for the motile body is a thin, slimy mass of protoplasm, with many nuclei and no cell walls. The "naked" protoplasm, or plasmodium, may be yellow, violet, or other colors, depending on the species. It is sometimes branched or netlike and can flow, in amoeboid manner, over moist soil, leaves, and logs rapidly enough for its movement to be seen. Slime molds digest and absorb whatever food the protoplasm contacts. They produce beautifully sculptured spore cases (sporangia).

ALGA-LIKE FUNGI (Phycomycetes) include water molds, black molds (p. 34), downy mildews, and blights (p. 35). Some are saprophytic; some parasitic. Most of the 1,500 species in this group are branched, forming cottony masses of threads that absorb food from the materials in which they live. The mass of threads is the mycelium, and each thread is a hypha. These fungi are more likely to occur on vegetable than on animal matter, but they do not ordinarily attack wood.

WATER MOLDS occur most commonly in fresh water, but many live in moist soil. Most are saprophytes living on dead insects or other animals or on dead plants; a few are parasites.

Water molds reproduce asexually by forming spores that develop into new plants. The spores swim by waving their whiplike flagella. As they look and move like one-celled animals, they are called zoospores. Some water molds also reproduce sexually.

Water molds contribute to the carbon and nitrogen cycles in the same manner as decay bacteria, but have little value otherwise. Some species of Saprolegnia are a common pest on fish eggs and young fish in hatcheries. Aquarium fish often become covered with the whitish masses of these water molds. The molds can generally be killed by placing the fish temporarily in a gallon of water in which 2½ tablespoons of salt have been dissolved.

SAPROLEGNIA—A WATER MOLD

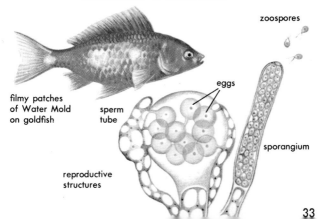

zoospores

filmy patches of Water Mold on goldfish

sperm tube

eggs

sporangium

reproductive structures

BLACK MOLDS include common bread mold and others that grow on overripe fruit, cheese, and other foods. Black molds get their name from their masses of black spores. A few species are parasites, some causing skin and eye diseases of man.

Bread mold is typical of all black molds. The air in any room may contain hundreds of thousands of its microscopic spores. If a spore falls on a piece of moist, fresh bread, it germinates and grows at a very rapid rate. The whitish mycelium develops quickly and branches out by extending runners (stolons). Tiny root-like structures (rhizoids) penetrate the bread and absorb food. Asexual reproduction is by tiny spores produced in rounded spore cases that split open to release their contents.

Bread mold spores are so light in weight they literally float in the air. Sex cells (gametes) are produced when hyphae of molds from opposite (+ and –) strains meet. Gametes unite to form a fertilized cell, or zygote, that develops a thick-walled spore case. Growth of mold spores in commercial bakery products is now inhibited by adding calcium propionate or similar chemicals.

Bread mold is generally saprophytic, but under some circumstances will grow as a parasite, on strawberries, for example.

Bread Mold
Rhizopus stolonifer

Asexual Reproduction

mycelium, with spore cases

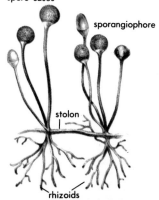

sporangiophore

stolon

rhizoids

Sexual Reproduction

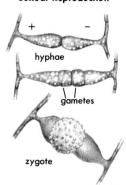

+   –

hyphae

gametes

zygote

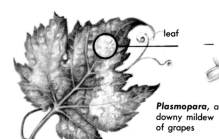

leaf

Plasmopara, a downy mildew of grapes

DOWNY MILDEWS cause serious diseases of crops, appearing as cottony spots on the leaves and stems of plants they parasitize. In grapes, the downy spots appear on the leaves, which change from pale green to yellow or brown as the mildew matures. The hyphae digest the epidermis of the grape leaf and penetrate the parenchyma tissues, absorbing the plant's juices and causing it to wilt. If the disease is not controlled, the leaves die and drop off. The grapes rot, and ultimately the plant dies. Control is by spraying with Bordeaux mixture (copper sulfate and lime).

Blights, such as the potato blight that devastated Ireland in 1845, are also caused by downy mildews. These alga-like fungi also cause fungus rot, a disease of beets and other vegetables. Many kinds attack seedlings, causing . roots to rot. Others grow into roots and stems at the soil line and cause a plant to wilt.

WHITE RUSTS are common on plants of the mustard family. All of the organisms can remain viable in the soil or on dead plant parts making control difficult.

Phytophthora, a downy mildew that causes late blight of potatoes

Albugo, a white rust on spinach leaf

35

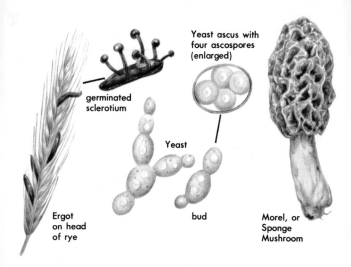

Yeast ascus with
four ascospores
(enlarged)

germinated
sclerotium

Yeast

Ergot
on head
of rye

bud

Morel, or
Sponge
Mushroom

SAC FUNGI (Ascomycetes), about 30,000 species, make up the largest class of fungi. They may be single-celled plants, as in yeasts, or of many cells in either a loose or a compact mycelium. They range in size from the microscopic to as much as 12 inches tall. All form a saclike reproductive structure, the ascus, that usually produces 8 spores. Yeasts reproduce also by budding.

Saprophytic sac fungi include *Penicillium*, yeasts, cup fungi, truffles, and morels. Many species live on organic matter in soils.

Parasitic sac fungi cause Dutch elm disease, powdery mildews, peach leaf curl, chestnut blight, ergot, and other diseases. The ergot fungus destroys such grains as wheat and rye, which are covered with a dark purple, poisonous mycelium, which in this case is called a sclerotium. Medicines used for treating mental disorders and for reducing hemorrhage are prepared from ergots.

Yeasts, important in the baking and brewing industries, derive their energy from sugar through fermentation. The end products of fermentation are carbon dioxide and alcohol. The carbon dioxide causes the bread to rise, and the small amount of alcohol evaporates during baking.

Cup fungi, morels, and truffles grow in moist humus, or decaying wood. The above-ground cuplike or sponge-like bodies grow from the mycelium network below. Spores are produced by these large fruiting structures. Morels and truffles are prized as food.

BLUE, GREEN, AND YELLOW molds are sac fungi that commonly grow on jellies, leather, fabrics, citrus, and other fruits. Some species of Penicillium spoil food; others are used in making Roquefort and Camembert cheeses. The blue patches in Roquefort are the spores. Penicillin, the antibiotic, was first prepared from Penicillium notatum but is obtained now from a more productive species. Another species, P. gresiofulvin, produces a substance that cures fungal skin diseases. One species of related genus, Aspergillus, is cultivated commercially to make citric acid; another species of Aspergillus causes a pulmonary disease.

Penicillium of different species is used by man in a variety of ways; to ripen cheese, for example.

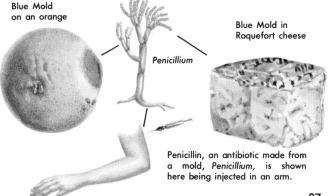

Blue Mold on an orange

Blue Mold in Roquefort cheese

Penicillium

Penicillin, an antibiotic made from a mold, Penicillium, is shown here being injected in an arm.

CLUB FUNGI (Basidiomycetes) include mushrooms, toadstools, puffballs, smuts, and rusts. All produce their tiny spores on knobbed or club-shaped structures (basidia). The 25,000 species of club fungi are the most advanced of the fungus groups. Mushrooms are the spore-producing bodies of underground mycelia that absorb food from decaying leaves or other organic matter. A "fairy ring" of mushrooms originates from a single underground mycelium that grows larger each year. "Fairy rings" may have a diameter of more than 100 feet. Each "fruiting" body, or mushroom, consists of a stalk and a cap. On the underside of the cap are gills—thin spore-bearing plates. Many mushrooms are edible, but there is no reliable rule of thumb for distinguishing the edible from the poisonous species.

Puffballs do not have caps or stalks. Young puffballs have a soft, white interior that is usually edible. When mature, puffballs are filled with spores that are released in a smokelike puff when the rind is ruptured.

Shelflike, woody brackets that grow on tree trunks are the reproductive structures of pore fungi. Spores escape through pores opening on the underside of the bracket. Many are found on living trees, and though they grow mainly in the dead wood cells, their enzymes may kill the living cells and eventually kill the tree. Some pore fungi closely resemble gill mushrooms.

Rusts and smuts are also parasitic fungi. Smuts, which have black spores, infect cereal crops. Rust fungi may require either one host or two alternate hosts. Black stem rust is perhaps the single most important plant disease; it parasitizes both wheat and barberry. White pine and currants or gooseberries are alternate hosts of white pine blister rust. Cedar-apple rust alternately infects cedar and apple trees. Rusts usually can be controlled by eliminating one of the two hosts.

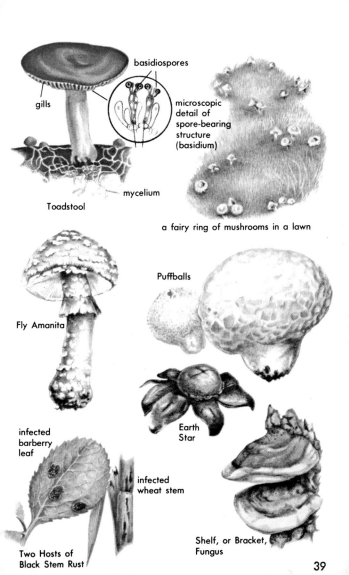

basidiospores

microscopic detail of spore-bearing structure (basidium)

gills

mycelium

Toadstool

a fairy ring of mushrooms in a lawn

Fly Amanita

Puffballs

Earth Star

infected barberry leaf

infected wheat stem

Two Hosts of Black Stem Rust

Shelf, or Bracket, Fungus

39

SYMBIOTIC FUNGI live in close association with other plants. This relationship is known as symbiosis. If both members of the partnership benefit, as in lichens (p. 41), the relationship is called mutualism. In a parasite-host relationship, one benefits at the expense of the other.

Some of the higher plants, such as pines, heaths, and orchids, lack root hairs and can grow successfully only if their roots are surrounded and penetrated by fungus filaments (mycorrhizae). This fungus-root relationship is an example of mutualism. The fungus filaments presumably increase the absorbing surface of the roots and may also make available to the plant various minerals from the soil that would otherwise remain unavailable. The fungus grows into the outer cells of its host's roots and gets its energy from the food stored there.

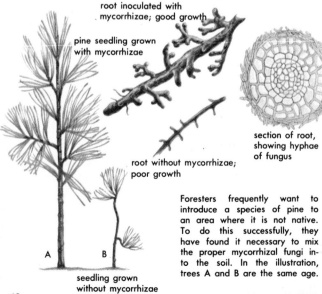

root inoculated with mycorrhizae; good growth

pine seedling grown with mycorrhizae

section of root, showing hyphae of fungus

root without mycorrhizae; poor growth

A   B

seedling grown without mycorrhizae

Foresters frequently want to introduce a species of pine to an area where it is not native. To do this successfully, they have found it necessary to mix the proper mycorrhizal fungi into the soil. In the illustration, trees A and B are the same age.

Some lichens grow tightly pressed against bark, rocks, or soil; this growth habit is crustose. Those adhering less closely to the surface have a foliose growth. Branched types that grow on land or hang from trees are classified as fruticose.

Usnea
a fruticose lichen

Parmelia
crustose lichen

Thallus section — alga
fungus filaments
rhizoid

Cladonia
fruticose lichen

Peltigera
foliose lichen

LICHENS form a group of plants in which numerous species of fungi, in both sac and club fungus groups, grow in partnership with simple blue-green or green algae. The algae are contained in a network of fungal threads, or hyphae. Food manufactured by the algae is shared with the fungus, which furnishes a protective, moisture-retaining habitat for the algae. The fungus and the alga reproduce by the methods characteristic of the individual species, or the entire structure may fragment and the pieces grow.

Lichens, which total about 15,000 kinds, are adaptable to meager environments and hence are widely distributed. They appear on barren, rocky areas and start the formation of soil in which mosses, then ferns and larger plants can grow. Lichens known as reindeer ''mosses'' furnish food for caribou in arctic areas. Litmus dye and a perfume stabilizer are made from lichens.

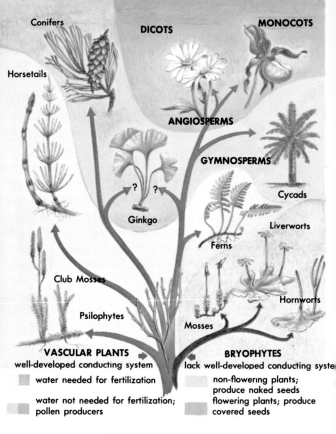

Conifers

DICOTS

MONOCOTS

Horsetails

ANGIOSPERMS

GYMNOSPERMS

? ?

Ginkgo

Cycads

Liverworts

Ferns

Club Mosses

Hornworts

Psilophytes

Mosses

VASCULAR PLANTS →
well-developed conducting system

water needed for fertilization

water not needed for fertilization;
pollen producers

BRYOPHYTES
lack well-developed conducting syste

non-flowering plants;
produce naked seeds

flowering plants; produce
covered seeds

EMBRYOPHYTES

This great group shows many adaptations for life on land. The development of pollen eliminates the need for water in fertilization. A waxy cuticle over stems and leaves prevents excessive water loss, as do the stomates that help control the exchange of water and air between the leaf cells and the atmosphere. Well-developed vascular systems permit rapid internal movement of water.

All of the Embryophytes produce a many-celled embryo that develops from the fertilized egg, or zygote. The life history is complex, an asexual, spore-producing generation (sporophyte) alternating with a sexual generation (gametophyte), as shown on p. 7. The two generations differ not only in appearance but also in number of chromosomes. In Bryophytes, the gametophyte is the dominant plant, and the sporophyte is mostly parasitic. In vascular plants, the sporophyte develops into the dominant, independent plant, on which the gametophyte is mostly parasitic.

ALTERNATION OF GENERATIONS requires a reduction in the number of chromosomes before sexual reproduction occurs. A mature sporophyte (1) develops spore mother cells (2) and then spores by a reduction division (meiosis) (3), in which each spore receives only n chromosomes, or half as many as in the sporophyte's $2n$ vegetative cells. After meiosis, the spores (4) germinate and produce gametophytes. Gametophytes (5) then produce sex cells, or gametes—eggs and sperms (6). When a sperm fertilizes an egg, the resulting cell, or zygote (7), has $2n$ or twice the chromosome number of a single gamete. The zygote develops into an embryo (8) that is at first parasitic on the female's gametophyte. In most vascular plants, the embryo is in the seed.

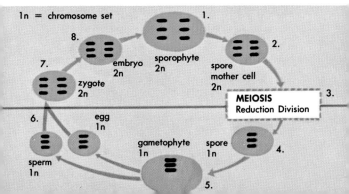

$1n$ = chromosome set

8.

7.

embryo $2n$

sporophyte $2n$

1.

2.

zygote $2n$

spore mother cell $2n$

MEIOSIS
Reduction Division

3.

6.

egg $1n$

gametophyte $1n$

spore $1n$

4.

sperm $1n$

5.

EMBRYOPHYTES WITHOUT SEEDS

BRYOPHYTES (liverworts, hornworts, and mosses) are small, green plants that prefer moist habitats, although most can tolerate seasonal drying. All produce gametes

HORNWORTS, as *Anthoceros*, have a simple gametophytic thallus. The horn-shaped sporophyte has stomates with guard cells like higher plants and, at its base, a meristem that enables it to continue growing in height. As spores mature, the apex splits to release them. The chloroplasts bear starch-storing pyrenoids.

LIVERWORTS, such as *Marchantia*, have a liver-shaped plant body, or thallus, with probably the first photosynthetic tissue

adapted for functioning on land. *Marchantia's* male and female gametophytes have sexual structures that differ, as shown. Sporophytes develop from fertilized eggs within the archegonia under the rays of the female sexual structure. Mature spores germinate to form new gametophytes, as do the asexual gemmae formed in cuplike structures on the upper surface of the thallus.

Porella, a "leafy" liverwort, has stalked antheridia and urn-shaped archegonia that may develop on the same plant.

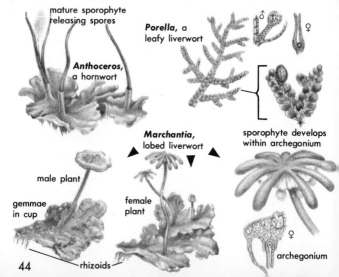

mature sporophyte releasing spores

Anthoceros, a hornwort

Porella, a leafy liverwort

♂   ♀

sporophyte develops within archegonium

Marchantia, lobed liverwort

male plant

gemmae in cup

female plant

♀

archegonium

rhizoids

44

in multicellular sex organs. Sperms swim through water to fertilize the egg which develops in its protective archegonium. Rootlike rhizoids grow from the conspicuous gametophyte plants on which the sporophytes are essentially dependent.

MOSSES are primary soil builders, growing on and spreading over bare surfaces. Haircap Moss illustrates the typical moss structure. Gametophytes are the free-living generations (see life cycle, p. 104). The sporophyte is usually green during development but becomes brown at maturity. Through a foot imbedded in the gametophyte, it obtains liquids and food as needed.

Sphagnums (bog mosses) are commercially important because of the great water-absorbing and holding capacity of dead cells.

Moss gametophytes have some features considered to be evolutionary in the change from living in water to life on land. Many appear to have stems, leaves, and roots, but only superficially like those of higher plants, since they lack vascular tissues. Moss protoplasm has the ability to survive drought. Shortly after a rain, dry and dead-looking moss will become green and active. Such features have helped make mosses successful as land plants; they occur profusely from the tropics to the poles.

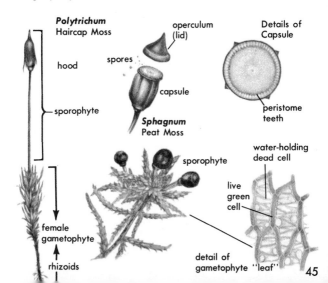

Polytrichum Haircap Moss

hood

sporophyte

spores

operculum (lid)

capsule

Sphagnum Peat Moss

Details of Capsule

peristome teeth

sporophyte

water-holding dead cell

live green cell

female gametophyte

rhizoids

detail of gametophyte "leaf"

45

Psilophytes in a Devonian landscape, from a reconstruction based on fossils 400 million years old.

PSILOPHYTES, once widely distributed, are rare plants today found only in isolated places. They are living examples of a primitive, once much larger group. These primitive plants lack true roots and have only scalelike leaves or none at all. Their vascular tissues—xylem, for conducting water and mineral solutions from the soil; and phloem, for transporting food—were and are still relatively simple systems. These adaptations produced a stiffened supporting stem that holds the plant upright.

Sporophytes of some extinct species, known only as fossils, are reconstructed above. Also shown are some low "strap-leaved" plants structurally intermediate between the algae and the vascular plants. *Psilophyton* had spiny stems, and the tips of its branches were coiled like fern "fiddleheads" (p. 50). *Rhynia* is regarded as an ancestral type from which other vascular plants probably arose. Its upright, leafless stems grew from creeping underground rhizomes. Spore cases developed at the tips of the aerial stems.

TMESIPTERIS, one of three living species of psilophytes, is found only in Australia and on adjacent Pacific Islands. It usually grows as an epiphyte on trunks of tree ferns. The leaves, while only about three quarters of an inch long, are still larger than those of *Psilotum* and have stomates in the epidermis; also have a definite midrib of xylem surrounded by phloem. The leaves shown here are slightly smaller than actual size.

PSILOTUM (Whisk Ferns) include two species, *P. complanatum* and *P. nudum*, that are widely distributed in the tropics and subtropics. Their branched green stems, about a foot tall, rise from horizontal stems called rhizomes. Buds formed on the rhizome will grow into new stems.

The leaves of *Psilotum* are mere small, pointed scales scat-

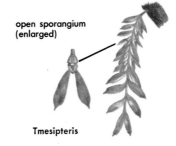

open sporangium
(enlarged)

Tmesipteris

tered along the aerial branches; the epidermis lacks stomates.

The sporangia are borne in clusters of three at the ends of very short lateral branches. Germinating spores develop into small gametophytes that grow underground and produce both eggs and sperms in many-celled sex organs. Gametophytes lack chlorophyll and appear to obtain nourishment through association with mycorrhizal fungi.

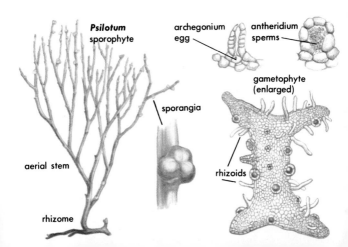

Psilotum
sporophyte

aerial stem

rhizome

sporangia

archegonium
egg

antheridium
sperms

gametophyte
(enlarged)

rhizoids

CLUB MOSSES AND QUILLWORTS have true roots, stems, and leaves, all with well-developed vascular tissue. Coal-forming carboniferous plant deposits were composed mostly of now-extinct tree-size members of this plant group. Unlike the ancient forms (p. 134), modern species are relatively small. Most of the 1,200 species require a damp, shady, tropical habitat.

LYCOPODIUMS have only one size spore, with terminal, club-shaped spore-bearing cones that suggest the name Club Moss. The vegetative leaves are small and single-veined, with stomates and photosynthetic tissues. The vascular tissue varies in arrangement but is largely of the primitive central core type.

ISOETES (quillworts) are semiaquatic plants. Because of fossil evidence and their kind of life cycle, quillworts are placed with the club mosses.

SELAGINELLA produces spores in two sizes. The smaller spores (microspores) develop into sperm-producing microgametophytes. The egg-producing megagametophyte develops within the larger spore (megaspore) while still retained in its megasporangium, as in seed plants. This suggests a possible link between these primitive plants and modern seed bearers.

Some species of *Selaginella* and *Lycopodium* look alike. They can be separated on the basis of cone and spore differences; *Selaginella* is more evolved.

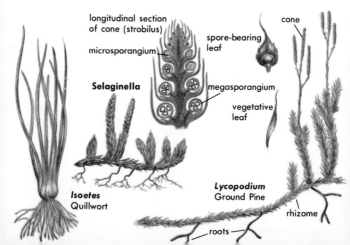

longitudinal section of cone (strobilus)

microsporangium

Selaginella

spore-bearing leaf

cone

megasporangium

vegetative leaf

Isoetes
Quillwort

Lycopodium
Ground Pine

rhizome

roots

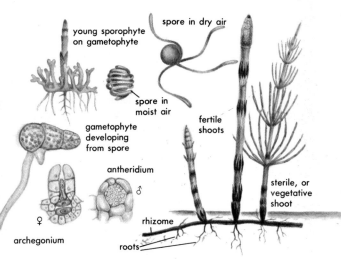

young sporophyte
on gametophyte

spore in dry air

spore in
moist air

gametophyte
developing
from spore

fertile
shoots

antheridium

♂

sterile, or
vegetative
shoot

rhizome

♀

roots

archegonium

Life cycle of common horsetail, *Equisetum*

HORSETAILS flourished in the swamps in Carboniferous times. Giant species of *Calamites* grew nearly 100 feet tall. The few living species (about 25) are remnants of this larger group; all belong to the genus *Equisetum*. The sporophyte, the dominant stage, is an herbaceous plant, most species growing along roads and in wet meadows.

The erect stems of horsetails grow from underground rhizomes that bear roots. The ribbed stems are hollow between the joints. Whorls of scalelike leaves grow from sheaths that surround each joint. The brushy sterile, or vegetative, shoots of some species give the plants the name horsetail. Spores are formed in strobiles at the tips of fertile shoots.

Some horsetail stems are rough and abrasive due to silica deposits in the epidermis. The stems of these so-called scouring rushes were used for cleaning pots and pans in colonial days.

FERNS, about 10,000 species, have conspicuous sporophytes with large, showy leaves, their veins equally branched. A typical fern leaf, or frond, has a stalk, or petiole, and an expanded blade. Some are undivided (entire), but in most, the blade is broken into leaflets. Fern leaves develop from "fiddleheads" that uncoil at the tip as they grow. In some ferns, spore cases (sporangia) commonly occur in clusters, or sori, on the underside of the leaves or leaflets. Others have special sporebearing leaves, leaflets, or spikes.

Some ferns grow in the open and in rocky or dry soils. A few are aquatic. Typically, however, ferns are found in moist soil and shade. In the tropics, where ferns are most abundant, many grow as epiphytes on trees and a few as climbing vines. Ferns from varied habitats and with a variety of growth habits and sporebearing structures are shown here. *Marsilea* is a rooted aquatic fern; *Salvinia*, a floating aquatic. The woodland Walking Fern forms new plants wherever a leaf tip touches the soil. Shield, Maidenhair, Adder's Tongue, and Interrupted Ferns are also woodland species. The grasslike Shoestring Fern is an epiphyte on tree trunks. Tropical Tree Ferns may grow to a height of 60 feet, with leaves 6 to 8 feet long. (Life cycle is on p. 105.)

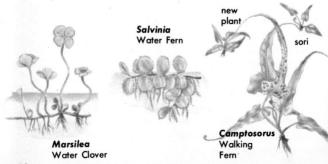

Salvinia
Water Fern

new plant

sori

Camptosorus
Walking Fern

Marsilea
Water Clover

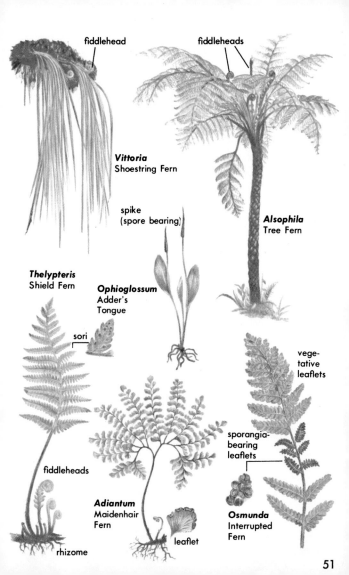

fiddlehead

fiddleheads

Vittoria
Shoestring Fern

Alsophila
Tree Fern

spike
(spore bearing)

Thelypteris
Shield Fern

Ophioglossum
Adder's
Tongue

sori

vegetative
leaflets

sporangia-
bearing
leaflets

fiddleheads

Adiantum
Maidenhair
Fern

leaflet

Osmunda
Interrupted
Fern

rhizome

EMBRYOPHYTES WITH SEEDS

Seed plants have an obscure origin, but evidence of seedlike structures occur on fossil plants of the early Coal Ages. Many of these plants—the seed ferns—looked like ferns but had "seeds" rather than spore cases on their leaves. Others resembled modern conifers. In seed plants, the seed-bearing sporophyte is dominant; the gametophyte is an inconspicuous parasite on the sporophyte.

Seeds appear to have evolved following the development of two types of spores: large megaspores (female) and small microspores (male). The seed develops from the megaspore containing a megasporangium, or ovule. A mature seed consists of an embryo that is frequently surrounded by a food reserve (endosperm) and a protective coat. Microspores develop into pollen grains that are transported to the ovules by wind, insects, or other means to bring about fertilization [pp. 108–109].

leaf of *Emplectopterus*, a seed fern (restoration)

Cordaites

EARLY SEED PLANTS included the seed ferns, such as *Emplectopterus* shown here. Seed ferns became extinct, but other seed-bearing plants of the Mesozoic (65–230 million years ago) survived and gave rise to the modern gymnosperms (p. 53) and angiosperms (p. 56). *Cordaites*, an early gymnosperm, may be the ancestral stock of modern cone-bearing plants. Fossils of the earliest angiosperm-like plants are about 200 million years old. Fossils with characteristics of modern angiosperms are found in rocks about 125 million years old.

seeds

branch with cones (strobili)

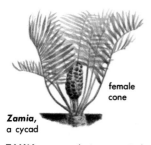

Zamia,
a cycad

female
cone

seeds

Ginkgo

ZAMIA, a cycad, is a tropical and subtropical palmlike evergreen that produces male and female cones on separate plants. Fossil cycads are known from as far back as the Triassic.

GINKGO, or Maidenhair Tree, is the only surviving species of a gymnosperm group that was widespread about 150 million years ago. Seeds develop from ovules produced on long stalks.

GYMNOSPERMS (about 700 species) include four extant orders: Coniferales, Cycadales, Ginkgoales, and Gnetales. Gymnosperms are woody plants that bear "naked" seeds: that is, not enclosed in an ovary. Most gymnosperms grow to tree size, but some of the primitive cycads, such as *Zamia,* have underground stems.

WELWITSCHIA, one of three very peculiar plants of the Gnetales order, grows only in the desert of southwest Africa. It never produces more than two leaves, which battered by windstorms become very tattered. The plant may live for centuries. *Ephedra, Gnetum,* and *Welwitschia* share some features with angiosperms.

PODOCARPUS, "foot fruit", belongs to a group of Coniferales in which the seed is associated with an aril, a fleshy outgrowth from the ovule stalk. The ovule structure is a modified cone.

Podocarpus

Welwitschia

staminate
cones

seed

aril

53

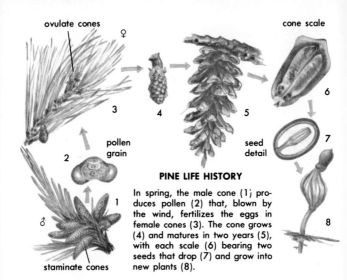

ovulate cones ♀

cone scale

3

4

5

6

pollen grain

seed detail

7

2

1

PINE LIFE HISTORY

In spring, the male cone (1) produces pollen (2) that, blown by the wind, fertilizes the eggs in female cones (3). The cone grows (4) and matures in two years (5), with each scale (6) bearing two seeds that drop (7) and grow into new plants (8).

8

♂

staminate cones

CONIFERS, such as pines, firs, cedars, spruces, and redwoods, form the largest group (about 500 species) of living gymnosperms. They are most abundant in cold and temperate regions. Nearly all conifers have needle-like or scalelike leaves and bear male and female cones on the same tree. Unlike the more primitive gymnosperms, conifers do not have motile sperms. Instead, the male cells are in pollen grains that are spread by the wind. In most conifers the seeds develop on cone scales. Conifers are classified mainly by types of cones and by the number and placement of their leaves.

Conifers furnish about 75 percent of the world's lumber and most of its pulpwood. Some Coast Redwoods are over 350 feet tall. A Montezuma Baldcypress near Oaxaca, Mexico, with a trunk diameter of 36 feet is believed to be 4,000 to 5,000 years old, as are some of the small Bristlecone Pines in the Southwest.

FAMILIES OF CONIFERS

ARAUCARIACEAE: large trees of the Southern Hemisphere; big cones and seeds, branches commonly whorled. Two genera.

CEPHALOTAXACEAE: shrubs or trees with short-stalked fleshy seeds and small, evergreen needles. One genus, Japan and Southeast Asia.

CUPRESSACEAE: shrubs and trees, mostly with flattened branches and scalelike leaves, opposite or whorled. The 16 genera, widely distributed, include cedars, junipers, cypress, and arborvitae.

PINACEAE: mostly trees, with woody cones and needle-like leaves in clusters. The 10 genera, found mainly in Northern Hemisphere, include pines, firs, spruces, hemlocks, Douglas-fir, larches, and true cedars.

PODOCARPACEAE: trees and shrubs; leaves needle-like or flattened, usually spiraled. Cone scale bearing seed usually fleshy. Mostly Southern Hemisphere; includes 7 genera.

TAXACEAE: small to medium-sized trees with seeds surrounded by a fleshy aril. Five genera, mainly in Northern Hemisphere, include yews and torreyas.

TAXODIACEAE: mostly trees, with needle-like or scalelike leaves and small, woody ,cones. Asia and North America; 10 genera, including sequoias, baldcypresses, and dawn redwood.

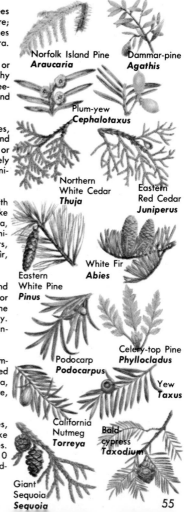

Norfolk Island Pine
Araucaria

Dammar-pine
Agathis

Plum-yew
Cephalotaxus

Northern White Cedar
Thuja

Eastern Red Cedar
Juniperus

Eastern White Pine
Pinus

White Fir
Abies

Podocarp
Podocarpus

Celery-top Pine
Phyllocladus

Yew
Taxus

California Nutmeg
Torreya

Bald-cypress
Taxodium

Giant Sequoia
Sequoia

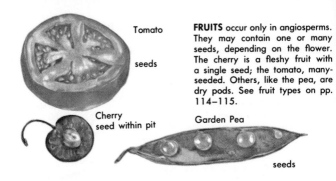

Tomato

seeds

Cherry
seed within pit

Garden Pea

seeds

FRUITS occur only in angiosperms. They may contain one or many seeds, depending on the flower. The cherry is a fleshy fruit with a single seed; the tomato, many-seeded. Others, like the pea, are dry pods. See fruit types on pp. 114–115.

ANGIOSPERMS (flowering plants) have flowers and bear seeds enclosed in a protective covering, or a fruit, that develops from the flower ovary and sometimes other flower parts (pp. 107–115). The type of flower, seed, and fruit is usually distinctive for each family. In angiosperms some of the xylem cells enlarge greatly, lose their end walls, and join, forming vessels. These vessels do not occur in most gymnosperms.

Flowering plants, the most recently evolved and the dominant plants today (about 250,000 species), include woody trees, shrubs, and vines, but the majority are herbaceous. Angiosperms are divided into two classes: dicotyledons (p. 58), in which the embryos have two seed leaves; and monocotyledons (p. 59), in which the embryos have one seed leaf.

GROWTH HABITS, structure, size, and range vary greatly in angiosperms. Some of these variations are shown on the next page. Peas, corn, and many others are annuals, bearing seeds and dying in one growing season. Biennials, such as carrots and celery, produce seeds at the end of the second growing season, then die.

Perennials flower and produce seeds repeatedly year after year. Woody perennials—trees, shrubs, and vines—commonly grow for several years before they flower for the first time. Some bamboos may grow vegetatively for as long as 60 years before they flower, produce seeds, and then wither and die.

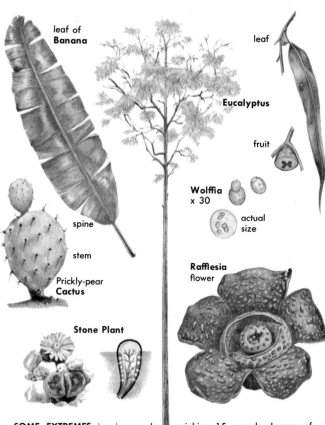

leaf of **Banana**

Eucalyptus

leaf

fruit

Wolffia x 30

actual size

spine

stem

Prickly-pear Cactus

Rafflesia flower

Stone Plant

SOME EXTREMES in sizes and growth habits of angiosperms are shown here. Australian eucalyptus trees, the giants of the group, grow to 300 ft.; smallest is the rootless aquatic *Wolffia*, no bigger than a pinhead. *Rafflesia*, a parasite on stems and roots of other plants, has the largest flower—up to 3 feet across and weighing 15 pounds. Leaves of some bananas grow 10 to 12 feet long and 3 feet wide, while those of most cacti are tiny (½ in.) or lacking. Cacti carry on photosynthesis in the outer, green layer of their thick stem. Stone plants grow almost completely buried in desert sand. A transparent cover lets light into leaf.

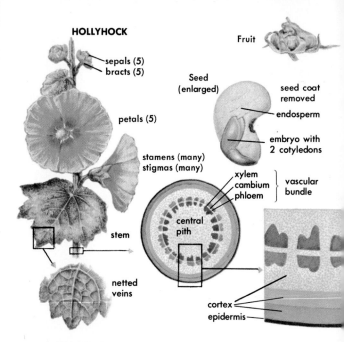

HOLLYHOCK

sepals (5)
bracts (5)

petals (5)

stamens (many)
stigmas (many)

stem

netted veins

Fruit

Seed (enlarged)

seed coat removed
endosperm

embryo with 2 cotyledons

xylem
cambium
phloem } vascular bundle

central pith

cortex
epidermis

DICOTYLEDON embryos have two seed leaves, or cotyledons. Flower parts are usually in fours or fives, and
the vascular tissues of the stem are arranged in a ring
of bundles surrounding a central pith. The leaves have
branching, netlike veins. Dicotyledons increase their
girth regularly by a division of the cambium cells.
Secondary thickening produces bark on perennial plants.
Examples of dicots include deciduous trees and shrubs,
like maples and lilacs; broadleaf evergreens, such as
magnolias and live oaks; roses, geraniums, and other
flowering perennials; tomatoes and most vegetables;
and weeds, such as dandelions and hawkweeds. There
are about 200,000 species of dicotyledons.

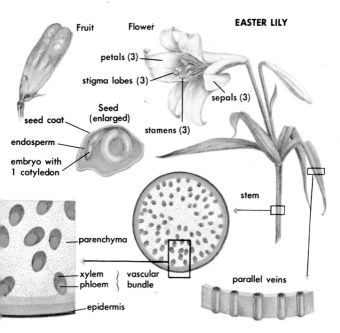

Fruit

Flower

EASTER LILY

petals (3)

stigma lobes (3)

sepals (3)

Seed
(enlarged)

seed coat

stamens (3)

endosperm

embryo with
1 cotyledon

parenchyma

stem

xylem
phloem } vascular
bundle

epidermis

parallel veins

MONOCOTYLEDON embryos have only one seed leaf, or cotyledon. They usually have narrow leaves with parallel veins. The bundles of vascular tissues are distributed throughout the stem's large, thin-walled parenchyma cells. A cambium is lacking in most monocots so they do not become woody. However some do have a special type of wood-like growth. In grasses and some other monocots, the stems are hollow except at nodes. Flower parts are in threes or in multiples of threes. This is the smaller of the two classes of flowering plants; it includes orchids, grasses, grains, lilies, palms, rushes, arums, and their allies. There are more than 50,000 species of monocotyledons.

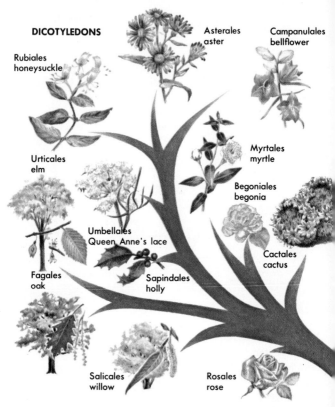

DICOTYLEDONS

Asterales
aster

Campanulales
bellflower

Rubiales
honeysuckle

Urticales
elm

Myrtales
myrtle

Begoniales
begonia

Umbellales
Queen Anne's lace

Fagales
oak

Sapindales
holly

Cactales
cactus

Salicales
willow

Rosales
rose

DICOTYLEDON RELATIONSHIPS are shown in the above chart of 24 important groups or orders. Most botanists believe that all dicotyledons evolved from a primitive kind of buttercup. The most recently evolved groups are shown toward the top of the two main divisions, with the order containing asters (Compositales) considered the most advanced.

A complete chart of living dicots would include about 250 families. Many characteristics are considered in determining evolutionary relationships. Morphological features, such as the number, size, and shape of plant parts, are important, as are the anatomical details of conducting tissues and other vegetative parts.

Special attention is given to flowers and seeds—to the form of the ovary, calyx, corolla, pollen, and embryo. Relationships are also shown by the number and shape of the chromosomes and by biochemical analysis of alkaloids or other unique compounds. Studies of fossil plants and of the geographical distribution of plants are also important.

Studies may show that plants differing greatly in size, form, and growth habit are nevertheless closely related. In the rose order are such trees as apple, pear, and cherry, as well as roses, strawberries, and other small herbaceous plants. While they differ in general appearance, examination of their flower parts reveals their kinship.

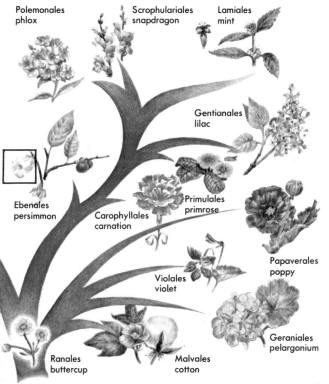

Polemonales
phlox

Scrophulariales
snapdragon

Lamiales
mint

Gentianales
lilac

Ebenales
persimmon

Carophyllales
carnation

Primulales
primrose

Papaverales
poppy

Violales
violet

Geraniales
pelargonium

Ranales
buttercup

Malvales
cotton

MONOCOTYLEDONS

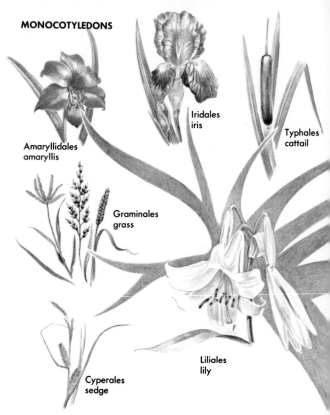

Iridales
iris

Typhales
cattail

Amaryllidales
amaryllis

Graminales
grass

Liliales
lily

Cyperales
sedge

MONOCOTYLEDON RELATION-SHIPS of the most common orders are shown above. Monocotyledons, like dicots (pp. 60–61), are believed by many botanists to have evolved from dicots, perhaps from a primitive buttercuplike ancestor; but the pattern of their evolutionary development is not completely known.

The grass family, with about 4,500 species, is one of the largest and possibly the most important plant family economically. Included are cereal grains (wheat, barley, rye, oats, corn, and rice) as well as sugar cane, and bamboos. The orchid family, containing more than 10,000 species, is the most highly specialized.

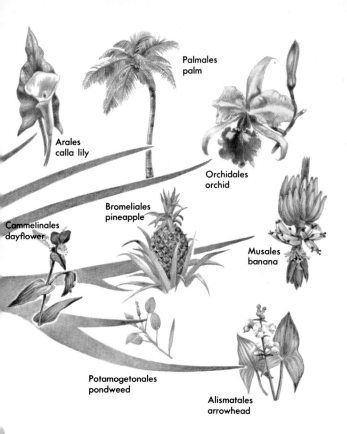

Palmales
palm

Arales
calla lily

Orchidales
orchid

Bromeliales
pineapple

Cammelinales
dayflower

Musales
banana

Potamogetonales
pondweed

Alismatales
arrowhead

Classification of plants is complicated because of the vast amount of data involved. Fossil records indicate that flowering plants have been evolving for about 150 million years. In this time they have diverged and changed in great degree from the ancestral stock. New evidence is being uncovered. Scientists are using computers to help organize this information. As knowledge of fossil and living plants increases, continued revisions of the arrangement and evolutionary placement of plant groups has become both possible and necessary. Several systems are in use today, and all are undergoing change.

ROOTS, stems, and leaves reach their greatest complexity in structure and function in the angiosperms. Roots anchor the plant in the soil, but their main role is to absorb water and dissolved minerals that are needed by the plant in the manufacture of food and for other uses. Food, especially starch, may be translocated and stored in the roots and is the main source of energy for growth at their tips. Root tissues are similar to those of stems, but root systems occur below ground. Shoot systems (stems and leaves) occur above ground.

A YOUNG ROOT lengthens rapidly by continual cell division and elongation near its tip. In this way it contacts new soil areas daily. The dividing cells also form a thimble-like protective cap over the tip.

Just behind the tip, the cells stop dividing, become longer, and begin to mature. In this region the epidermal cells develop root hairs, through which water and minerals are absorbed. In effect, the root hairs increase the absorption surface of a root by 5 to 20 times.

The root hairs bend and twist as they grow around the soil particles. Root hairs are gradually sloughed off and new ones produced as the root tip grows. Competition with other plants influences both the lateral and vertical extent of root systems.

Young Root

Enlarged portion of root hair zone with root hairs (single cells) pushing through soil

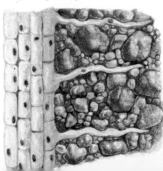

zone of
maturation

root hairs

zone of
elongation

zone of
cell division

root cap

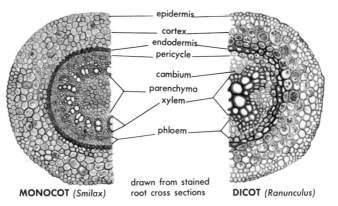

epidermis	
cortex	
endodermis	
pericycle	
cambium	
parenchyma	
xylem	
phloem	

MONOCOT (Smilax)   drawn from stained root cross sections   **DICOT** (Ranunculus)

MATURE ROOTS are usually cylindrical in cross section. The single outer layer of cells, the epidermis, protects the underlying tissues. Immediately beneath is the cortex, composed mostly of large thin-walled cells (parenchyma) with numerous interspaces. Water and gases diffuse easily through these loosely arranged cells, which also store foods. Inside the parenchyma, a single layer of cortex cells (endodermis) controls the direction of water movement. Branch roots originate from the next inner layer of cells, the pericycle.

A dicotyledon root differs from a monocotyledon root mainly in having a cambium layer. Xylem cells instead of parenchyma cells occupy the root's center. Older dicotyledon roots may become woody.

ROOT SYSTEMS of many plants grow deeper and spread wider than the height and spread of the plant above ground. Alfalfa roots, for example, may extend 25 feet down in a two-year-old field and have been found as deep as 130 ft. in mine shafts. Roots of Common Mesquite have been found in a pit mine 175 feet deep. Measurement of a single rye plant revealed almost 14 million roots; combined length, about 380 miles; total surface area, 2,500 square feet, roughly 50 times more than the plant's stems and leaves.

USDA

STEMS are the connecting link between the roots and leaves. They support the leaves and are the transportation route along which water and dissolved minerals move to the leaves and down which food travels from them (p. 68). Stems are often used to propagate new plants by vegetative reproduction (non-sexual process).

Young Twig

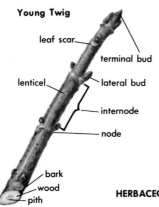

leaf scar

terminal bud

lenticel

lateral bud

internode

node

bark
wood
pith

YOUNG STEMS are commonly green and carry on photosynthesis. Like leaves, these are covered with a protective coat, the cuticle, that limits water loss through their surface. Stems may be classified as herbaceous (non-woody) or woody.

In winter many stems are leafless. Buds, lenticels, and bark color, peculiar for each species, aid identification. Twigs of many woody plants show successive bud-scale scars marking annual increments in length.

HERBACEOUS STEMS

MONOCOT stem conducting cells occur in bundles that lack cambium. These bundles are distributed throughout the stem. No well-defined pith area occurs, but some have a central "pith cavity" that makes them hollow. Monocot stems ordinarily do not grow in diameter; dicot stems do.

DICOT stem conducting cells consist of many bundles that contain cambium. These form a definite ring around the pith. Growth in diameter begins when a ring of cambium forms by bridging from bundle to bundle. Woodiness develops as xylem cells accumulate.

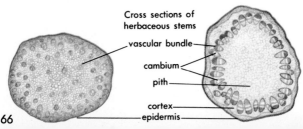

Cross sections of herbaceous stems

vascular bundle

cambium

pith

cortex
epidermis

Stems are usually conspicuous and easily distinguished from the roots and leaves. Some, however, are very short and hidden under a crown of leaves, as in beets and carrots. Others grow underground (rhizomes and tubers), serving also in asexual reproduction. Modified stems include thorns and vines.

WOODY STEMS of dicotyledons and gymnosperms increase in diameter due to divisions of cambium cells during many growing seasons. Cells developed from the cambium on its outer side become the phloem tissue; end walls are perforated with sievelike openings.

Cork cambiums developed in the outer phloem produce waterproof cells. These together with all phloem make up the bark.

Cells produced on the inside of the cambium develop into xylem. Vessels are formed from xylem cells that lose their contents and end walls, forming long tubes through which water moves easily. Other common xylem cells are known as tracheids and fibers.

As new xylem cells are produced, both the cambium and phloem are displaced outward, and the stem increases in diameter. Commonly, large xylem cells form in early spring; smaller ones in summer. This pattern of different-sized cells makes annual rings that can be counted to determine a tree's age.

WOODY STEM

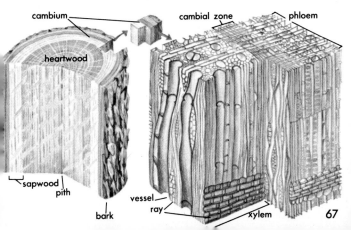

GREEN LEAVES usually have a thin, broad blade that affords a maximum surface for light to penetrate the green cells. Most photosynthesis takes place here. The vein meshwork is the leaf's rigid, supporting skeleton, as well as its system of conduction.

A leaf consists of various tissues: an epidermis covering the upper and lower surfaces; a middle layer, or mesophyll; and the conducting tissues that form the veins. Xylem occupies the upper part of the veins; phloem, the lower part. The veins transport raw materials, water, and products of photosynthesis.

THE MESOPHYLL consists of cells between the two epidermal layers. Except for the veins, these cells contain chlorophyll, hence are food makers. Typically, cells at the top are tall and cylindrical, forming the palisade layer. Cells below the palisade layer are irregular in shape and have large spaces between them. They form a spongy layer through which carbon dioxide and oxygen move.

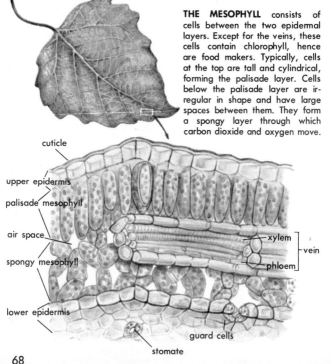

cuticle

upper epidermis

palisade mesophyll

air space

spongy mesophyll

lower epidermis

xylem

phloem

vein

guard cells

stomate

THE EPIDERMIS, both upper and lower, usually consists of a single layer of tightly fitting cells that do not contain chlorophyll. It is covered with a waxy coat, the cuticle, that helps to prevent excessive loss of water.

STOMATES are pores that occur abundantly in the lower epidermis and in much lesser number in the upper epidermis. Stomates are characteristic of Embryophytes; are unknown in the Thallophytes. A single oak leaf may contain as many as 350,000 stomates. Carbon dioxide and oxygen pass in and out through these pores. Water that is evaporated in transpiration (p. 79) also passes out through the stomates.

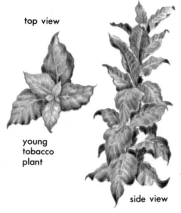

top view

young tobacco plant

side view

LEAVES are arranged around the stem in a definite order, or phyllotaxy, so that each leaf gets a maximum exposure to the light.

TWO GUARD CELLS surround each stomate. Unlike the other epidermal cells, the guard cells contain chlorophyll and can manufacture food. This is thought to be associated with their ability to control the size of the opening. By day they have a concentration of sugar that causes water to diffuse into them from surrounding cells. The wall of a guard cell is thick on the side toward the pore. On the opposite side it is thin. Due to the intake of water, the cell swells on its thin-walled side, and the thick wall on the pore side bows toward the thin wall. This opens the pore. At night, when photosynthesis stops, the sugar content of the guard cell drops. As the cell's excess water diffuses into the surrounding cells, the pore closes.

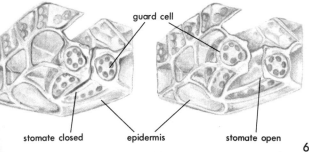

guard cell

stomate closed   epidermis   stomate open

69

Plants, like animals, need energy for growth, reproduction, and tissue repair. Foods are the source of this energy. All plants that possess chlorophylls (or their equivalent) manufacture food by photosynthesis. Solar energy is necessary in the process, hence the sun is the basic source of energy for all living things. Plants produce more food than they utilize and become directly or indirectly the food supply of all animals.

ENERGY is received, stored, and transferred between the molecules of living cells by two phosphate compounds: adenosine diphosphate (ADP) and adenosine triphosphate (ATP). These high-energy compounds are formed of adenine (a nitrogen compound), ribose (a sugar), plus phosphates.

The addition of a phosphate group to ADP can be compared to charging a battery. ATP, with three phosphates, is fully charged. When one of these phosphates is removed, energy is made available for work. Some ATP is produced during photosynthesis, but most of it is formed during respiration (p. 84).

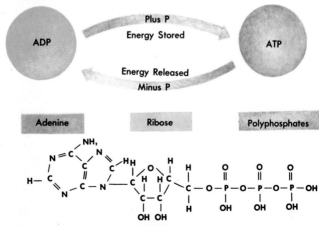

C–carbon, N–nitrogen, H–hydrogen, O–oxygen, P–phosphorus,

PHOTOSYNTHESIS converts solar energy into chemical energy through the action of light and chlorophylls *a* and *b*. Raw materials entering the process are water and carbon dioxide. End products are sugar, oxygen, and water.

A very small percentage of the solar energy falling on the plant is utilized in photosynthesis. Yet this chemical process annually combines some 25 billion tons of hydrogen with about 150 billion tons of carbon to produce about 300 billion tons of sugar. About 400 billion tons of oxygen are released in the process. About 80 percent of all photosynthesis takes place in marine algae or phytoplankton.

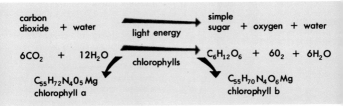

carbon dioxide + water → light energy → simple sugar + oxygen + water

$$6CO_2 + 12H_2O \xrightarrow[\text{chlorophylls}]{} C_6H_{12}O_6 + 6O_2 + 6H_2O$$

$C_{55}H_{72}N_4O_5Mg$
chlorophyll a

$C_{55}H_{70}N_4O_6Mg$
chlorophyll b

CHLOROPHYLLS, the green pigments contained in chloroplasts (p. 72), act as solar energy absorbers and are involved in the changing and transferring of energy until the energy finally is stored in the sugar molecule. The chlorophyll molecule links energy from the sun with all life on earth. Chlorophylls *a* and *b* are the most common of the several kinds of chlorophylls that differ from each other in chemical composition. Note the different amounts of hydrogen and oxygen in the chemical formulae for chlorophylls *a* and *b* above.

Such external factors as temperature, light intensity, and availability of water and carbon dioxide affect the rate of photosynthesis. Most plants carry on photosynthesis over a wide temperature range—from 50 to 100 degrees F. For a few, the optimum is above or below these extremes. Nitrogen and magnesium also occur in the chlorophyll molecule, but the elements iron, potassium, phosphorus, and zinc are believed also to be essential in chlorophyll formation. The details of the photosynthetic process are much the same in all green plants.

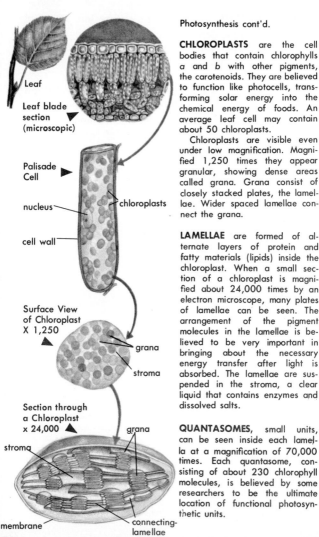

Photosynthesis cont'd.

CHLOROPLASTS are the cell bodies that contain chlorophylls *a* and *b* with other pigments, the carotenoids. They are believed to function like photocells, transforming solar energy into the chemical energy of foods. An average leaf cell may contain about 50 chloroplasts.

Chloroplasts are visible even under low magnification. Magnified 1,250 times they appear granular, showing dense areas called grana. Grana consist of closely stacked plates, the lamellae. Wider spaced lamellae connect the grana.

LAMELLAE are formed of alternate layers of protein and fatty materials (lipids) inside the chloroplast. When a small section of a chloroplast is magnified about 24,000 times by an electron microscope, many plates of lamellae can be seen. The arrangement of the pigment molecules in the lamellae is believed to be very important in bringing about the necessary energy transfer after light is absorbed. The lamellae are suspended in the stroma, a clear liquid that contains enzymes and dissolved salts.

QUANTASOMES, small units, can be seen inside each lamella at a magnification of 70,000 times. Each quantasome, consisting of about 230 chlorophyll molecules, is believed by some researchers to be the ultimate location of functional photosynthetic units.

Leaf

Leaf blade section (microscopic) ▶

Palisade Cell ▶

nucleus

chloroplasts

cell wall

Surface View of Chloroplast X 1,250 ▶

grana

stroma

Section through a Chloroplast x 24,000 ▶

grana

stroma

membrane

connecting-lamellae

72

LIGHT REACTIONS, which take place in the grana, are one of the two groups of chemical processes that alternate in the photosynthetic cycle. When a photon of light strikes an electron in a chlorophyll molecule, the chlorophyll is "activated," and the electron is raised to a higher energy level. Electrons from these activated chlorophyll molecules split water molecules into hydrogen and oxygen-hydrogen components. The electrons and hydrogen atoms are received by hydrogen-acceptor compounds, and oxygen is given off. In splitting water, some ATP is produced. Finally the chlorophyll molecule is returned to its original inactive state; it is not used up in the process.

DARK REACTIONS may occur either in light or in dark but do not require light energy directly. They utilize carbon dioxide, plus the hydrogen of the acceptor compounds and the ATP from the light reactions. The carbon dioxide gains an activated sugar molecule with only 5 atoms of carbon to make a 6-carbon sugar molecule. This molecule changes again and forms glucose, a common simple sugar. Water is also produced. The hydrogen-acceptor compounds and the ADP in the process are then available again for another light reaction. Both reactions require only fractions of a second, but a light reaction is many times faster than a dark reaction.

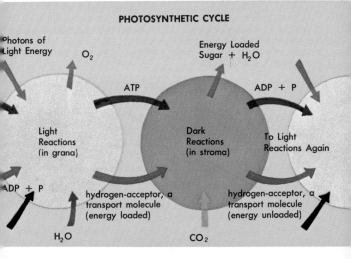

PHOTOSYNTHETIC CYCLE

Photons of Light Energy

O_2

Energy Loaded Sugar + H_2O

ATP

ADP + P

Light Reactions (in grana)

Dark Reactions (in stroma)

To Light Reactions Again

ADP + P

hydrogen-acceptor, a transport molecule (energy loaded)

hydrogen-acceptor, a transport molecule (energy unloaded)

H_2O

CO_2

AUTOTROPHIC NUTRITION is characteristic of most plants. For growth, they need only inorganic substances and an energy source. If light is the energy source, the plant is known as a photoautotroph. If a chemical reaction is the energy source, the plant is a chemoautotroph.

Bacteria are usually heterotrophs (p. 76), but two exceptions, the photosynthetic and chemosynthetic bacteria, are described below.

PHOTOSYNTHETIC BACTERIA possess bacterial chlorophylls and other pigments. Bacterial chlorophyll has minor chemical differences from the chlorophyll of other plants; however, like green plants, photosynthetic bacteria require solar energy.

Most common of the photosynthetic bacteria are the purple sulfurs. In photosynthesis, they use hydrogen sulfide rather than water as a hydrogen source, and they deposit sulfur in their cells instead of releasing oxygen.

Non-sulfur purples use organic substances rather than sulfur compounds in photosynthesis.

CHEMOSYNTHETIC BACTERIA, important in the nitrogen cycle (p. 145), secure energy by oxidizing simple compounds of hydrogen, nitrogen, sulfur, or iron. They contain no chlorophyll and can live independent of light.

Several kinds of bacteria get energy by changing soluble iron compounds into insoluble compounds. A common rod-shaped type forms a twisted band of iron hydroxide around its cell. Concentrations of iron by such bacteria may be responsible for some of the world's major iron deposits. Some iron bacteria can oxidize manganese as well.

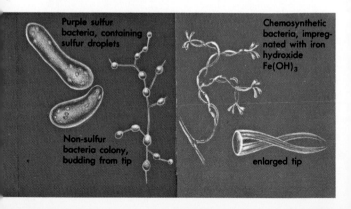

Purple sulfur bacteria, containing sulfur droplets

Non-sulfur bacteria colony, budding from tip

Chemosynthetic bacteria, impregnated with iron hydroxide $Fe(OH)_3$

enlarged tip

The carnivorous plants below are photoautotrophs with an unusual ability to supplement their nutrition. These plants trap insects and other small animals and "digest" them. From the digested bodies they obtain usable nitrogen as well as other chemicals that are frequently deficient in their bog habitat. Only small animals are trapped, so stories of man-eating plants are pure fabrication.

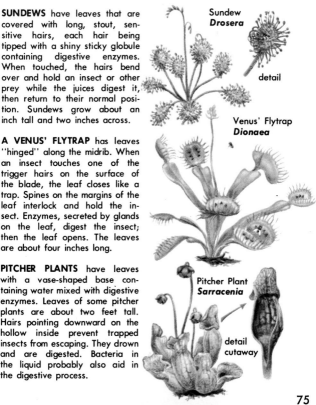

Sundew
Drosera

detail

Venus' Flytrap
Dionaea

Pitcher Plant
Sarracenia

detail
cutaway

SUNDEWS have leaves that are covered with long, stout, sensitive hairs, each hair being tipped with a shiny sticky globule containing digestive enzymes. When touched, the hairs bend over and hold an insect or other prey while the juices digest it, then return to their normal position. Sundews grow about an inch tall and two inches across.

A VENUS' FLYTRAP has leaves "hinged" along the midrib. When an insect touches one of the trigger hairs on the surface of the blade, the leaf closes like a trap. Spines on the margins of the leaf interlock and hold the insect. Enzymes, secreted by glands on the leaf, digest the insect; then the leaf opens. The leaves are about four inches long.

PITCHER PLANTS have leaves with a vase-shaped base containing water mixed with digestive enzymes. Leaves of some pitcher plants are about two feet tall. Hairs pointing downward on the hollow inside prevent trapped insects from escaping. They drown and are digested. Bacteria in the liquid probably also aid in the digestive process.

75

HETEROTROPHIC NUTRITION is characteristic of plants that must have external sources of organic substances for growth. These substances can be obtained from dead or from living plants and animals. Plants dependent on the dead for their nutritional needs are saprophytes; those that depend on the living are parasites. Some plants may obtain nutrition either way, depending on conditions. Most plants can be classified on a nutritional basis, though in some cases this is not easy.

soft tissues
of citrus leaf
decay soon
leaving only
vein network

Coral Root Orchid
Corallorrhiza

Snow Plant
Sarcodes

Indian
Pipe
Monotropa

SAPROPHYTIC BACTERIA AND FUNGI begin to cause the decay of plants and animals immediately after their death. Their action eliminates organic litter and returns elements and compounds to food and energy cycles. Decay of soft mesophyll cells of a leaf may occur after a leaf falls. The veins decay later.

CORAL ROOT ORCHIDS lack chlorophyll. They grow in rich, moist soils, from which their fleshy rootstocks absorb organic matter. They are assisted by mycorrhizal fungi that surround the roots, absorbing water and mineral salts. Most orchids, in contrast, are green and can manufacture their own food.

SNOW PLANTS flower in early spring in the mountains of western U.S. Often they appear before the last snows. Snow Plants are closely related to the widely distributed Indian Pipe. These plants are peculiar saprophytes in their dependency on mycorrhizal fungi to obtain their food from the rich forest humus. The relationship may be a form of mutualism.

In Indian Pipe, for example, the exact nutritional relationship of the mantle of mycorrhizal fungi (p. 40) to the plant's root and to the organic substances in the soil around it is not clear. Mistletoe is commonly classified as a parasite. It is photoautotrophic (p. 74) but is dependent on its host for water and minerals. Some call it a partial parasite. By use of radioactive markers some of the sugars produced in the mistletoe leaves are found to be translocated to the host.

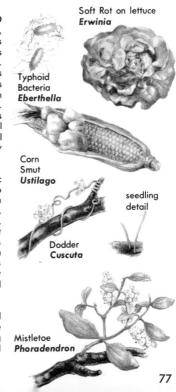

Soft Rot on lettuce
Erwinia

Typhoid Bacteria
Eberthella

Corn Smut
Ustilago

seedling detail

Dodder
Cuscuta

Mistletoe
Phoradendron

PARASITIC BACTERIA AND FUNGI are common. Soft rots, crown galls, and fire blights are among the many plant diseases caused by parasitic bacteria. Smuts, mildews, rusts, and blights (pp. 33–35) are fungus parasites of plants. Fungi cause Dutch elm disease and chestnut blight.

Bacterial and fungus parasites are responsible for many animal diseases. Typhoid is a bacterial disease. Ringworm is caused by a fungus parasite.

DODDER, one of the few parasitic flowering plants, is related to morning glories. The yellowish plant, which lacks chlorophyll, grows from seed as a slender, threadlike leafless stem that elongates until its tip touches and coils around the stem of a host plant. Then it produces modified roots (haustoria) that penetrate the host plant and absorb food and water.

MISTLETOES are only partial parasites. They can manufacture food, but lack roots, obtaining the raw materials, water and minerals, from their host.

FOODS—carbohydrates, fats, and proteins (pp. 79–81) used by plant cells in growth and repair as in animals—are all dependent on sugar production by photosynthesis. The annual food production by plants is enormous—2 to 3 tons on an average woodland acre, 30 to 35 tons per acre in fields of sugar cane.

The soluble sugar is moved from the cells in the leaves where it is made to other parts of the plant for storage or modification. It is generally changed into starch, an insoluble carbohydrate (p. 79), or into fats or proteins (pp. 80–81). The chemical reactions necessary for these changes are controlled by enzymes in the cells. Enzymes are mostly complex molecules of protein that can act to bring about very complicated chemical changes without damage to the cells.

FOOD STORAGE STRUCTURES

Leaves

Fruits

Stems

Roots

Flower Head

Seeds

Structural Formula for
Glucose $C_6H_{12}O_6$

OH
H – C – H
C
H O H
C C
OH OH H OH
C C
H OH

Glucose and Fructose
are combined to
form the more complex
sucrose molecule

$$C_6H_{12}O_6 + C_6H_{12}O_6 \xrightarrow[\text{enzyme}]{\text{energy}} C_{12}H_{22}O_{11} + H_2O$$

glucose   fructose   sucrose   water

CARBOHYDRATES—such as sugars, starches, and cellulose—are compounds of carbon, hydrogen, and oxygen.

Glucose, a simple sugar, may be used directly in respiration (p. 84) or may be transported, changed into other compounds, and stored. Sucrose, a more complex sugar, is a common form of storage sugar. It is formed by a reaction between glucose and fructose.

Starches, which are insoluble in water, are the most common form of carbohydrate storage. Starch grains are distinctive in shape. The starch molecules are composed of long, coiled or spiraled chains of simple sugar molecules.

During the day, some of the excess glucose being produced in the leaf is transformed immediately into starch and stored temporarily in the chloroplasts. When photosynthesis stops with darkness, this starch is changed into glucose, moved in solution to other parts of the plant, and deposited again as starch.

Cellulose is made of many glucose sugar molecules linked together, forming fibrous bundles. It is the principal constituent of cell walls but is not used as a food in the plant in which it is formed. Many fungi, however, do digest cellulose in their nutritional processes. This is the cause of wood decay.

Starch grain at left is intact; at right, it is partly digested, the chains broken by removal of oxygen link.

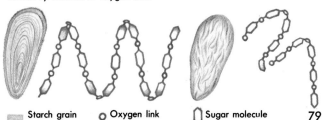

Starch grain   o Oxygen link   Sugar molecule   79

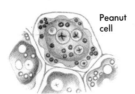

Peanut cell

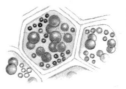

Coconut meat

▲ Oil   ▲ Protein   ▲ Starch

FATS AND OILS contain carbon, hydrogen, and oxygen, like carbohydrates, but the proportion of hydrogen to oxygen is greater. At normal temperatures fats are solids; oils are liquids. Both are insoluble in water. They appear as droplets in protoplasm or in cell vacuoles.

Fats are rich sources of energy, one gram of fat yielding twice as much energy as a gram of a carbohydrate. Many seeds and nuts are rich in fats and oils as well as in protein.

Fats are built in the plant by joining one molecule of glycerol with three molecules of fatty acids.* Waxes, which form the thin, protective cuticle over leaves and stems, are related compounds in which the glycerol has been replaced by alcohol molecules.

Vegetable oils, such as those obtained from the fruit of olives and from the seeds of coconut, oil palm, peanut, and cotton, are important to man both as food and for other purposes. Oleomargarine and cooking oils are modern uses of plant oils as foods. Coconut and palm oils are used in quantity for soap production. Linseed oil, prepared from flax seed, has the unusual property of forming films when exposed to air. Oil paints owe their protective coat to this oil.

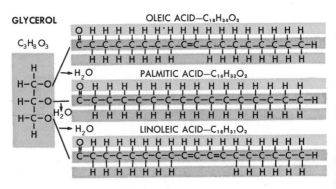

GLYCEROL $C_3H_8O_3$

OLEIC ACID—$C_{18}H_{34}O_2$

PALMITIC ACID—$C_{16}H_{32}O_2$

LINOLEIC ACID—$C_{18}H_{31}O_2$

*One molecule of water (H_2O) is split off by each union (3 HOH's lost)

80

PROTEINS, the largest and most complex of the food molecules, are the chief constituents of protoplasm. They are found also in enzymes, in cell membranes, and in chloroplasts. In seeds they are commonly stored as granules.

The basic units in proteins are amino acids, about 20 of which are considered essential to life. Glycine, the simplest amino acid, contains carbon, hydrogen, oxygen, and nitrogen. A few of the more complex amino acids also contain sulfur. Each kind of protein consists of particular kinds, numbers, and sequences of the 20 amino acids. They occur in long chains, linked end to end and usually in a complex and definite shape.

ELEMENTS that are essential in plant nutrition number about 16 of the 105 known. Those needed in larger quantities include carbon, hydrogen, oxygen, nitrogen, sulfur, phosphorus, potassium, magnesium, iron, and calcium. Six trace elements also are now considered essential: boron, cobalt, copper, manganese, molybdenum, and zinc. Most are obtained from the soil; others are added to soils in commercial fertilizers. Leaf, or foliar, analysis is now widely used as a means of detecting nutritional deficiencies, excesses, and imbalances in plants, thus helping to guide soil fertility.

Fertilizers are not plant foods, but are raw materials containing essential elements that living cells can incorporate into their protoplasm. Only living cells can accumulate elements in solution. To get fertilizer salts into solution, a film of water must exist between the soil particles in which a plant's roots are growing. The salts move by diffusion through this water to the roots.

Blueberry Leaf: Foliar Symptoms of Element Deficiencies

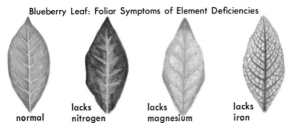

normal | lacks nitrogen | lacks magnesium | lacks iron

WATER is necessary for photosynthesis, respiration, digestion—and also for the movement of foods and minerals. For each pound of plant material produced, wheat needs about 60 gallons of water; potatoes, about 80; and corn, 40. An acre of corn takes in more than 300,000 gallons of water from the soil each season, but only about 2 percent is retained and used.

Arrows indicate direction of water movement

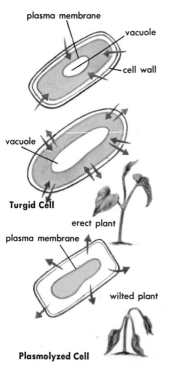

plasma membrane

vacuole

cell wall

vacuole

Turgid Cell

erect plant

plasma membrane

wilted plant

Plasmolyzed Cell

OSMOSIS involves diffusion, or spread, of molecules of a liquid or gas from an area of greater concentration to one of less. The movement is through a semipermeable membrane. A cell membrane permits some molecules to pass through but not others. Movement of water into a plant's roots occurs largely by osmosis.

TURGOR increases as cells take in more water by osmosis and imbibition (p. 83). A turgid cell actually bulges, its cell vacuole is so filled with water the cytoplasm pushes the cell membrane against the cell wall. Turgor keeps stems of herbs erect and accounts for some plant movements. Guard cells around stomates open due to turgor, increasing transpiration.

PLASMOLYSIS, the opposite of turgor, is the shrinkage of cytoplasm from the cell wall. This occurs when salts or soluble foods (sugars) are in greater concentration outside than inside the cell. As a result, water moves out of the cell by osmosis, and the cytoplasm shrinks away from the wall. Killing weeds by placing salt around their roots involves this process.

82

Water moves into and through a plant by the processes described below and on facing page. Measurements show that an active absorption of water occurs at a rate faster than can be explained by osmosis and imbibition. Active absorption of water (requiring respiration), still not full understood, occurs only in living cells and requires expenditure of some energy.

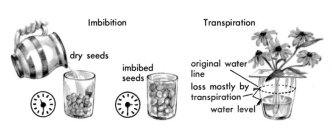

Imbibition

dry seeds

imbibed seeds

Transpiration

original water line

loss mostly by transpiration

water level

IMBIBITION is the soaking up of water by cell walls and by other organic substances. The pressures developed by imbibition are tremendous, strong enough to rupture thick seed coats. The Egyptians drove wooden wedges into cracks in rocks, soaked the wedges, and imbibitional swelling split the rocks.

TRANSPIRATION is the evaporation of water from the aerial parts of plants. Two kinds are recognized: stomatal (accounting for most) and cuticular, which occurs through the waxy covering of leaves and stems. The process is controlled in part by turgidity of the guard cells (p. 69). Evaporation of water from the leaf in transpiration helps prevent the leaf from overheating in the sun. Water lost through the leaves is replaced through the root system.

Water loss by transpiration can be excessive and cause the death of a plant. Because transpiration cannot be completely controlled, plants survive only when an adequate and continuous supply of water is in the soil. If too much water floods the soil, the roots suffer from lack of oxygen, life processes stop, and no water intake occurs. The plants wilt.

Plants are variously adapted to moisture extremes. The roots of some, such as cattails, get oxygen from the leaves. The plants thrive in water. At the other extreme, desert plants have small leaves with thick cuticles and protected stomates. These adaptations help reduce transpiration in the desert and allow survival even with very limited rainfall. Water uptake must balance loss by transpiration.

RESPIRATION is a complex series of chemical reactions, involving many different enzymes, that releases the chemical energy of foods. All living cells depend on this process to provide the energy needed for their life processes (p. 10). Thus, respiration must occur continuously, day and night, in all living things.

Respiration in most plants is aerobic, utilizing free oxygen from the air in completely oxidizing the food (mainly carbohydrates and fats). Aerobic respiration gives a high energy yield. In anaerobic respiration, no free oxygen is utilized, and the amount of energy released is low. Some higher plants may survive for short periods by anaerobic respiration. Yeasts and some bacteria may live by anaerobic respiration alone.

MITOCHONDRIA are the cell structures in which respiration occurs, just as chloroplasts are the site of photosynthesis. These small, colorless rod-shaped or spherical bodies are scattered through a cell's cytoplasm.

Electron microscopes reveal that each mitochondrion is surrounded by a double membrane. The outer membrane covers the mitochondrion smoothly. The inner membrane has many folds that effectively increase its surface and allow for proper positioning of the several respiratory enzymes. These enzymes in the mitochondria control the chemical reactions in respiration. Enzymatic control prevents the build-up of high temperatures that would be destructive to the cells.

Energy Exchange

mitochondria

Nutrients — proteins
carbohydrates
fats

CO_2

PO_4
ADP
O_2

outer membrane
inner membrane

H_2O

ATP
energy for metabolism

84

GLYCOLYSIS is the process by which glucose, the simple sugar, is broken down into two smaller molecules of pyruvic acid in a number of separate chemical steps. Glycolysis does not require oxygen and is the first step in both aerobic and anaerobic respiration.

Sugar must be made chemically active before glycolysis can begin. This is accomplished by the addition of two high energy phosphate bonds, utilizing ATP previously produced by respiration. At the end of the process, however, there is a net gain of ATP since more is produced in glycolysis than is used.

ANAEROBIC RESPIRATION releases only part of the potential chemical energy of a food. A common example is the alcoholic fermentation of sugar by yeasts. Some bacteria are strictly anaerobic surviving in oxygen free environments.

In yeasts, the pyruvic acid molecules formed in glycolysis are changed to carbon dioxide and ethyl alcohol, in which most of the energy of the original food remains, plus a small amount of ATP. Carbon dioxide, formed as yeast cells respire, causes dough to rise in baking. Yeast fermentation is also the basis of brewing, wine making, and several important chemical industries. Respiration of acetic acid bacteria is fundamental in making vinegar. Lactic acid bacteria, which produce no carbon dioxide, are utilized in souring processes in the cheese and dairy industries and in making sauerkraut.

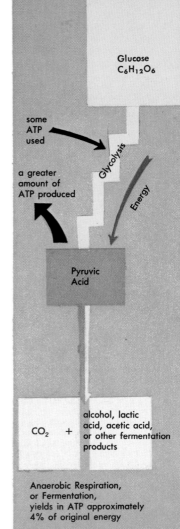

Glucose
$C_6H_{12}O_6$

some ATP used

Glycolysis

a greater amount of ATP produced

Energy

Pyruvic Acid

CO_2 + alcohol, lactic acid, acetic acid, or other fermentation products

Anaerobic Respiration, or Fermentation, yields in ATP approximately 4% of original energy

85

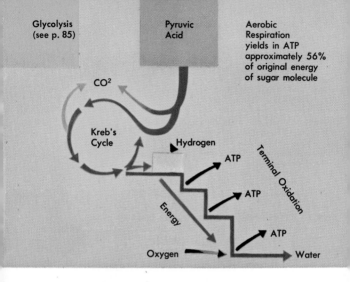

Glycolysis (see p. 85)

Pyruvic Acid

Aerobic Respiration yields in ATP approximately 56% of original energy of sugar molecule

CO^2

Kreb's Cycle

Hydrogen

ATP

Terminal Oxidation

Energy

ATP

ATP

Oxygen

Water

AEROBIC RESPIRATION is an oxidizing process, a kind of slow "burning" in which the temperature is controlled by enzymes in the mitochondria (p. 84). Energy is released. Thus aerobic respiration is essentially the chemical reverse of photosynthesis in which energy is stored.

In aerobic respiration, the pyruvic acid molecules resulting from the glycolysis of sugar (p. 85) lose some carbon as carbon dioxide and then become involved in the Kreb's cycle, a complicated series of chemical reactions that proceed stepwise, releasing small packets of energy. The Kreb's cycle reactions may in some cases also be the initial steps in the synthesis of fats or proteins. Or fats and proteins may be digested, and the re-

sulting smaller molecules will enter into the Kreb's cycle and be respired, releasing their energy.

The energy transfer in Kreb's cycle is accomplished by electrons being passed from one molecule to another—in concept, like the flow of electric current through a wire.

The end products of aerobic respiration are carbon dioxide, water, and energy that is stored temporarily as high-phosphate bonds of ATP. The ATP moves through the cell cytoplasm and releases its energy by transfer of the phosphate groups to other compounds as needed for repair or for growth movements (such as cytoplasmic streaming). As ATP loses one of its phosphates, it becomes ADP which goes back into the respiratory cycle again.

TRANSLOCATION OF SUGAR in plants occurs in water solutions. Neither diffusion nor streaming of cytoplasm through the cell can account for the speed with which sugar molecules travel. Differences in osmotic concentration creating a pressure flow system may be partly responsible. For this system to work, green cells in the leaves act as sugar producers. In non-green cells in the roots and in some leaf and stem cells, the sugar is converted to starch and stored. Phloem and xylem (p. 9) connect the leaf and root cells; thus a sort of circuit is completed for the circulation of sugar and water.

Glucose marked with radioactive carbon has been shown to move three feet per hour in stems. The direction of movement is always toward the area of maximum use. Movement of molecules from cell to cell may occur through very small connections of cytoplasm (plasmodesmata) that run through cell walls.

MOLECULES moving from cell to cell pass through cell membranes that are selectively permeable. This prevents the cell's molecules from leaking out as water and salts enter.

Soluble foods also pass from cell to cell through these membranes, which are a living part of each cell. ATP provides the energy needed in some of these transfers. Enzymes are probably involved also.

Under an electron microscope, these unit membranes appear as a pair of fine parallel lines with a clear area between. The lines are believed to consist of protein molecules; the clear area to be a complex fat (phospholipid) containing phosphorus and nitrogen. A varying amount of stretching of the protein molecules may control the size of the pores and thus controls which soluble food molecules can pass through.

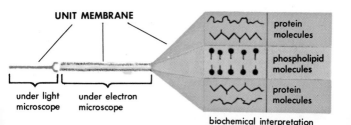

UNIT MEMBRANE

under light microscope | under electron microscope

protein molecules
phospholipid molecules
protein molecules

biochemical interpretation

Plants respond in a variety of ways to stimuli in their environment. Movement, growth, and flowering are common reactions. They are all incompletely understood and are subjects of current research. Light, gravity, and contact are among the stimuli that bring about these reactions, but no response can be explained as a direct result of a single stimulus. Many stimuli at work simultaneously play a part in a plant's growth and development.

GROWTH MOVEMENTS are usually slow but are permanent (nonreversible). They are frequently called tropisms. A response to gravity, for example, is a geotropism; to light, a phototropism; to touch, a thigmotropism.

Hormones (p. 90) are generally involved in the process. Roots or stems bend because the cells on their opposite side grow unequally. This is brought about by a difference in the distribution of growth hormones.

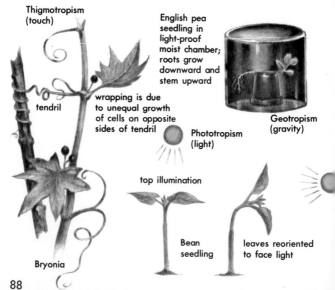

Thigmotropism (touch)

English pea seedling in light-proof moist chamber; roots grow downward and stem upward

tendril

wrapping is due to unequal growth of cells on opposite sides of tendril

Geotropism (gravity)

Phototropism (light)

top illumination

Bean seedling

leaves reoriented to face light

Bryonia

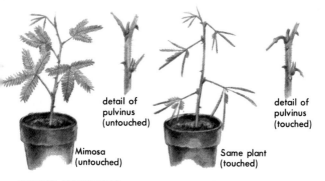

detail of pulvinus (untouched)

Mimosa (untouched)

Same plant (touched)

detail of pulvinus (touched)

TURGOR MOVEMENTS are usually rapid and are reversible, not permanent. When a Mimosa plant is touched (stimulated), cells in the enlargement (pulvinus) at the base of the leaflets and in the leaf petioles leak water into the spaces between the cells and thus lose their turgor pressure (p. 82), the normal tension due to fluids inside the cell. This causes the leaflets to fold and the leaves to droop—all within seconds. Recovery takes about 15 minutes. Mimosas are so sensitive that they were once suspected of having a nervous system, like animals.

Loss of turgor pressure causes Venus' Flytrap leaves to shut quickly (1–2 seconds) and trap an insect that has touched them. In many plants, as in the flower of the Sausage Tree, the lobed stigmas close and enclose pollen grains that have landed there. Turgor movements account for the sleep movements of Oxalis and of many clovers, peas, locusts, and other legumes. Their leaves are spread open to the sun during the day but close at night. The turning of a plant's leaves and flowers in following the course of the sun during the day appear also to involve turgor movements.

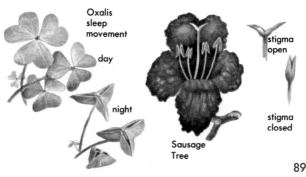

Oxalis sleep movement

day

night

stigma open

stigma closed

Sausage Tree

HORMONES are organic compounds that act as chemical messengers and help to coordinate plant activities. They are involved, for example, in the development of flowers and fruit and may either stimulate or inhibit growth. A hormone is produced in only small amounts and then is transported to another location where it exercises its control over some plant process. Concentrations as low as one part in a billion parts of water may be effective in some cases.

Since the discovery of natural plant hormones in 1928, many synthetic substances have been made that also affect growth and other plant processes. These growth regulators, a term that refers both to naturally produced and to synthetic compounds, are important tools in modern horticulture and agriculture.

AUXINS, best known of the plant hormones, occur in a plant's growing and developing parts—as in seeds, stem tips, fruits, young leaves, and buds. Light, gravity, and some kinds of chemicals influence their production and distribution. If light shines on only one side of a plant, more auxin is distributed to the dark side. This causes the cells there to elongate and curves the stem toward the light. In uniform light, the auxin is distributed in equal amounts on all sides, and the stems grow upright.

The amount of an auxin needed for normal growth is very small. Stem tips require more than do lateral buds or roots. Too much auxin disturbs a plant's balance of growth, and may cause death. This makes possible the use of growth regulators as weed killers.

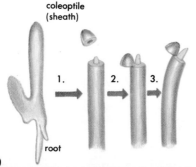

coleoptile (sheath)

1. 2. 3.

root

Auxin is produced by the tip of an oat sheath (coleoptile). When the tip is removed (1), and placed to one side (2), growth occurs as shown (3). The hormone diffuses down only one side, stimulating cell enlargement there and causing curvature.

GIBBERELLINS were first reported by Japanese botanists who were studying the "foolish seedling disease" of rice. They found that a parasitic fungus growing on the rice plant produced a hormone, Gibberellic acid, that caused the rice to grow abnormally tall.

Gibberellins are effective mainly on stems, and plants treated with very small amounts of gibberellins will grow many times taller than untreated plants. Treatment can be made by applying the hormone as an aerosol spray to the entire plant or by dabbing a small amount of a lanolin-gibberellin mixture on the plant's young stems.

Cabbage is a biennial that normally takes two years to produce its flowering stem, but plants treated with gibberellin flowered in one year. Non-vining bush beans will develop the vining habit if treated with the hormone gibberellin.

treated

untreated

KINETINS seem to be associated with auxins in controlling plant growth and development. The three flasks below contain tobacco tissues. All were given the same amount of auxin. The tissue in the flask with no kinetin developed neither roots nor buds. Those in the flask with a small amount of kinetin developed only roots; those in the flask with a larger amount developed buds also.

DORMINS belong to a group of plant hormones that inhibit growth and apparently provide a system of checks and balances in the hormone systems.

Other plant hormones are known, and probably many more will be discovered. Vitamins B_1 and B_2, both produced by leaves, are essential for root growth. Some plants also require nicotinic acid for root growth.

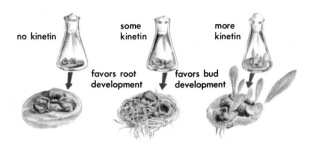

no kinetin

some kinetin

more kinetin

favors root development

favors bud development

PHOTOPERIODISM is the effect of day length (hours of light) on plant development, especially flowering. At the equator, day and night are of about equal length all year; in other latitudes, day length changes with the season. In some plants, temperature also plays a significant role. The phytochrome pigment (p. 95) and probably florigen, a hormone, are also involved in flowering.

Plants can generally be placed in one of three photoperiod classes: short day, long day, or day neutral. A long-day plant is one that will flower on day lengths longer than the critical minimum for the species. The critical day length for both spinach and red clover, for example, is 12 hours. These plants will flower only on days when there is light for 12 hours or more. A short-day plant flowers only when day lengths are shorter than the critical minimum for the species. Poinsettias are short-day species that also have a 12-hour critical day length. They flower only when they have light for less than 12 hours. Chrysanthemums, also short-day species, have a critical day length of 15 hours. A day-neutral species flowers regardless of day length. Recently matured leaves seem to be the best receptors for light. The red portion of the light is most effective in producing the flowering effect.

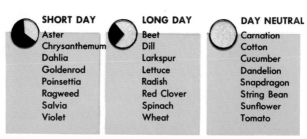

SHORT DAY
Aster
Chrysanthemum
Dahlia
Goldenrod
Poinsettia
Ragweed
Salvia
Violet

LONG DAY
Beet
Dill
Larkspur
Lettuce
Radish
Red Clover
Spinach
Wheat

DAY NEUTRAL
Carnation
Cotton
Cucumber
Dandelion
Snapdragon
String Bean
Sunflower
Tomato

**Salvia,
a short-day plant**

flowering

PLANT DISTRIBUTION is controlled in part by photoperiods. Short-day plants are common near the equator. Both short- and long-day species are found in temperate zones. Plants that grow at latitudes greater than 60 degrees, both north and south of the equator, are mostly long-day species. Day-neutral species occur at all latitudes. Short-day species usually flower in early spring, late summer, or fall. Long-day plants flower in late spring and early summer.

Florists can control the time of flowering by changing the length of day artificially. Short-day plants, such as chrysanthemums, can be kept from flowering in winter by using lights to extend the length of the short winter days. Short-day plants can be made to flower in long days of summer by covering them with a light-proof cloth in late afternoon. This permits "programmed flowering" to meet market needs.

flowering

**Lettuce,
a long-day plant**

PHOTORECEPTORS are necessary for the utilization of light energy in plant processes. These are the plant pigments that absorb particular wavelengths of light. The part of the electromagnetic radiation spectrum shown above includes the visible portion (390 to 760 millimicrons) which we see as white light and which also produces most of the responses studied in photobiology. These light waves are a part of every plant environment, and different wavelengths influence different growth processes. Three main groups of photobiological process are known: (1) responses of chlorophyll in photosynthesis (p. 71); (2) responses to blue and red light (below); and (3) responses of the phytochrome system (p. 95).

BLUE AND RED LIGHT are absorbed by the chloroplasts in photosynthesis. Both chlorophylls and carotenoids are the photoreceptors. Most of the energy for food synthesis comes from the red wavelengths. Blue light is responsible also for photo-tropisms. This is shown below where the plant stem bends and grows only toward the blue light. This bending is brought about by an adjustment of plant hormone balance (p. 90). The blue light photoreceptor appears to be beta carotene.

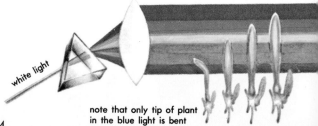

white light

note that only tip of plant
in the blue light is bent

PHYTOCHROME, first isolated in 1959, is a blue protein pigment that functions as an important photoreceptor. It is involved in systems that control photoperiodism, elongation of stems between nodes, formation of plant pigments (especially in the ripening of fruits), germination of seeds, and probably other processes as well.

Phytochrome exists in reversible forms, referred to by code numbers: P660, which has a light absorption peak in red light (660 millimicrons), and P730, which has a light absorption peak in far-red (730 millimicrons). If P660 is exposed either to sunlight or to red light, it changes to P730. If the P730 is then exposed to far-red light, it changes quickly back to P660. This change also occurs slowly in darkness.

Experiments with lettuce demonstrated that seeds of some varieties normally contain P660 and will not germinate unless exposed either to red light or to sunlight, changing the inactive P660 to the active P730. This explains why some seeds will not germinate if buried too deeply. But if the soil is turned and the seeds are thus exposed to light, they will then sprout. In this way their own food-manufacturing process begins before their stored seed food is exhausted. Normal growth is thus possible.

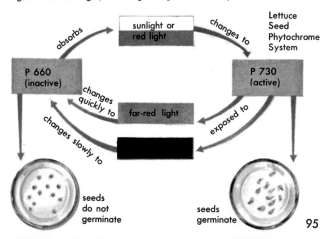

Lettuce Seed Phytochrome System

P 660 (inactive) — absorbs — sunlight or red light — changes to — P 730 (active)

P 730 (active) — changes quickly to — far-red light — changes slowly to — P 660 (inactive)

P 730 (active) — exposed to —

seeds do not germinate

seeds germinate

95

SOME PRACTICAL USES OF AUXINS, or their synthesized chemical equivalents (growth regulators), are important to horticulturists, florists, gardeners, orchardists, and others who depend on plant production and performance for their livelihood. Applied to plants, the auxins will produce their effects, sometimes accelerating and sometimes retarding growth.

ROOTING OF CUTTINGS. Heteroauxin, common in green plants, is indoleacetic acid (IAA). Produced synthetically, IAA is mixed with indolebutyric acid and other similar growth stimulators and applied to cuttings to promote rooting. This method is used in nurseries to propagate plants that do not root easily.

The effects of auxin vary in detail according to the species, the stage of growth, the environmental conditions, and the amount of dosage.

FOOD PRESERVATION may be extended in potatoes, onions, and other vegetables. They may be either sprayed or placed in a vapor of auxin-like substances to delay sprouting and prevent shrinkage for as long as a year. This holds their market value to a maximum.

If N^6 benzyl adenine is applied as a post-harvest dip, broccoli will keep longer and stay greener because the normal rate of chlorophyll loss is slowed down. These treatments can be used to supplement low temperature storage.

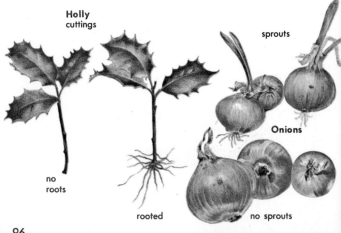

Holly cuttings

sprouts

Onions

no roots

rooted

no sprouts

WEED KILLERS, notably 2,4-D, are auxin-like substances that kill weeds by disturbing their normal growth. In small quantities, these auxins actually stimulate plant growth. In heavy concentrations, they kill. Most grasses are resistant to their effects, hence weed killers are used to destroy broadleaved weeds.

Dandelions in untreated grass (above); none in treated grass (below).

FRUIT DEVELOPMENT is stimulated by auxins that are ordinarily produced by developing seeds. If some of the egg cells in an apple flower are not fertilized, they fail to produce both seeds and auxins. The result is a misshapen apple, flattened on one side.

By applying auxin-like sprays, even unpollinated flowers can be made to produce well-shaped fruits which will be seedless. A normal and a hormone-treated tomato are shown here.

normal tomato— with seeds

hormone-treated tomato with no seeds

PREMATURE FRUIT DROP may be prevented by spraying the maturing fruit with auxin-like substances. Auxins produced by young fruits keep them firmly attached to the twigs. As the fruit matures, the auxin supply decreases, and cells at the base of the fruit stem disintegrate. Fruit often drops when these separation (abscission) layers develop prematurely. Spraying with auxin-like substances delays the formation of the abscission layer.

Auxin-like sprays are used also to delay the ripening of fruit for shipment and to prevent the production of flowering stalks ("bolting") in lettuce and similar leafy vegetables.

Apple tree unsprayed; fruit has dropped

sprayed; fruit develops

97

ENVIRONMENTAL CONTROL of the form and shape of plants can be observed in natural habitats. A knowledge of hormones and responses to stimuli makes it easier to understand the way plants grow.

geranium bending toward light

crown broken from tree   same tree 4 yrs. later

wound cavity   2 yrs. later

HOUSE PLANTS tend to grow toward the nearest window. This is a phototropic response in which hormone distribution is involved (p. 90). The plants must be rotated regularly to make them grow with uniform shape.

TREES that lose branches in ice or wind storms usually develop a smaller, more compact crown. Loss of the terminal buds removes the source of a hormone that usually suppresses growth of the lateral buds. In the plants' recovery, the lateral buds grow vigorously and give the trees their new appearance. This same mechanism causes pruned hedges to become bushier.

TREE WOUNDS are common, yet the trees continue to live. Wounded plant tissues produce traumatin, a hormone that causes cells of the cambium around the wound to reproduce rapidly and form a callus. New bark produced by the callus eventually covers the wound.

STREET TREES commonly respond to street lights near them. As the days get shorter in autumn, a photoperiodic response (p. 92) causes the leaves to turn color and eventually drop. But the leaves that are near street lights are in an artificially long day. They do not change color as soon, and they stay on the tree longer.

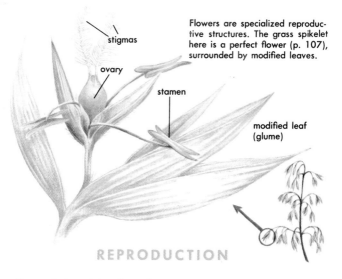

stigmas

ovary

stamen

Flowers are specialized reproductive structures. The grass spikelet here is a perfect flower (p. 107), surrounded by modified leaves.

modified leaf (glume)

REPRODUCTION

Every living thing has the capacity to reproduce—to form new individuals of its kind. In simple one-celled plants, reproduction consists of dividing to form two independent cells. When conditions are favorable, some bacteria divide about every 20 minutes, thus quickly building up an enormous population. In other lower plants and in some of the more advanced species, fragments of a plant may break off and form new individuals. In both of these methods the offspring are genetically identical to the parents.

In sexual reproduction, the offspring receive hereditary materials from two parents and thus bear traits of both. This results in the great variety that occurs among individual plants that reproduce sexually. The most advanced plants form seeds that permit a delay in the development of the new plant until environmental conditions are favorable for growth.

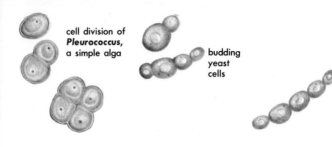

cell division of *Pleurococcus*, a simple alga

budding yeast cells

ASEXUAL REPRODUCTION is the development of a new plant from a single parent. It is restricted mainly to one-celled plants and involves either a division of single-celled plants into two or the production of spores. In yeast cells, a bud grows from the parent cell and eventually breaks off to grow independently. Filamentous algae may break into fragments, each continuing to grow and becoming a new filament. Some higher plants produce offspring vegetatively from their roots, stems, or leaves (p. 116). Some banana plants, for example, can reproduce in no other way.

ASEXUAL SPORES are often produced in large numbers. Wind or water may aid in distributing them. Many aquatic plants, such as *Vaucheria* below, produce spores that can swim (zoospores). Other spores are thick-walled, serving as a dormant stage in which plants survive such unfavorable conditions as cold or drought. In bacteria, the cell may simply develop a thick wall around itself, as in *Tetanus* shown below. In some plants, spores are produced in special structures (sporangia). When conditions are favorable, a spore germinates and grows into a new plant. *Saprolegnia*, a water mold, produces sporangia of this type.

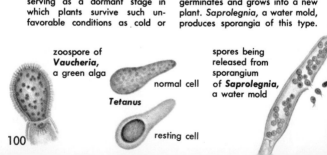

zoospore of *Vaucheria*, a green alga

normal cell

Tetanus

resting cell

spores being released from sporangium of *Saprolegnia*, a water mold

FISSION of *Gloecapsa*, a blue-green alga (no well-defined nucleus)

nucleus

MITOSIS in *Chalmydomonas*, a motile green alga

1. chromosomes divide into chromatids

2. chromatids separate; spindle forms

3. chromatids move to opposite poles

CELL DUPLICATION can occur in several ways. Fission involves a division of the nuclear material and surrounding cytoplasm. A constricting ring forms around the cell wall and grows inward, cutting the cell in two. How the cell's hereditary material (chromatin) is duplicated by this method is not fully understood.

Most cell division is by mitosis and cytokinesis in cells with a well-defined nucleus. In many-celled plants, mitosis increases the number of vegetative cells.

In mitosis, the chromatin is first organized into threads that become a definite number of chromosomes (p. 118). The nuclear membrane then disintegrates. Each chromosome has been duplicated to produce two chromatids. A spindle forms, and the chromatids separate and move toward opposite ends, or poles, in the cell. After the chromatids (now chromosomes) collect at the poles, each nucleus reorganizes. A plate develops at the center of the cell and grows outward to wall of the mother cell. The daughter cells have hereditary material identical to that of the parent cell and mature into cells like the parent cell.

4. chromatids (now chromosomes) reach the poles; **CYTOKINESIS** begins with formation of cell plate

5. chromosomes reorganize into nuclei

6. two daughter cells emerge from old cell wall

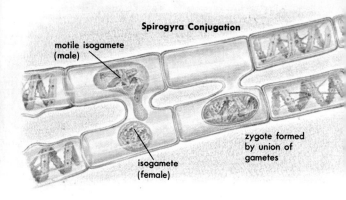

Spirogyra Conjugation

motile isogamete (male)

isogamete (female)

zygote formed by union of gametes

SEXUAL REPRODUCTION involves a union of two gametes. Gametes of some lower plants (as in *Spirogyra* above) look alike (isogametes). Their union is called fertilization. In most plants, the sex cells are of two different types (heterogametes). The smaller male gamete (sperm) swims; the larger female gamete (egg) is non-motile. The zygote formed by the union of these two sex cells contains the chromosomes present in each gamete. This diploid (2n) number of chromosomes is always the same for each species and is found in all of the plant's body cells. The diploid number must be divided in half by a reduction division, or meiosis, to arrive at the haploid (1n) number of chromosomes in the sex cells.

In some algae and fungi, meiosis occurs soon after the zygote forms, hence the plant exists with 2n chromosomes for only a short time. But in most plants the zygote and the cells formed from it divide by mitosis as the plant grows and enlarges, and the 2n number of chromosomes is maintained until sexual spores are formed. This may be a year or, as in most woody plants, many years later. Then meiosis occurs, reducing the chromosome number of the gametes to the haploid (1n) number.

MEIOSIS I
(1-5)

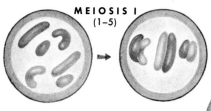

2. chromosomes with like determiners pair

1. mother cell with six chromosomes

MEIOSIS, or reduction division, involves two phases in the division of the nucleus:

In **Meiosis I** (1-5), all of the chromosomes come together and those with determiners for the same traits are paired. Each chromosome doubles, but the two halves remain attached. The double chromosome pairs separate and move to opposite ends of the cell.

In **Meiosis II** (6-8), a second chromosome division occurs, and the resulting four groups organize into nuclei. Thus, four nuclei are produced. In most plants that reproduce sexually, meiosis is one phase in an alternation of generations (p. 43).

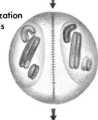

3. paired chromosomes double and align on equator

4. chromosomes move toward opposite poles

5. reorganization begins but is not usually completed

MEIOSIS II
(6-8)

8. cell divides to form 4 haploid cells

7. chromosomes move to poles

6. chromosomes align at equator

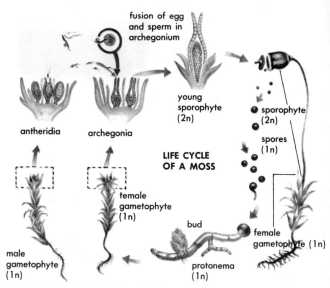

LIFE CYCLE OF A MOSS

fusion of egg and sperm in archegonium

young sporophyte (2n)

sporophyte (2n)

spores (1n)

antheridia

archegonia

female gametophyte (1n)

female gametophyte (1n)

bud

male gametophyte (1n)

protonema (1n)

REPRODUCTION IN MOSSES involves an alternation of a gametophytic with a sporophytic generation. The sex cells (gametes) are produced in many-celled sex organs, the archegonia (female) and antheridia (male). These are usually located in the tips of separate female and male gametophytes. The sperm leaves the antheridium, swims through a film of water, and unites with the egg in the archegonium. This produces the zygote that grows into a stalked sporophyte, its base embedded in the female gametophyte from which it obtains nourishment. At its tip, a sporangium develops in which spores are formed by meiotic division (p. 103). Each spore contains the haploid (1n) number of chromosomes. When expelled from the ripe sporangium, the spores germinate on damp soil. They form protonema, the buds of which become gametophytes.

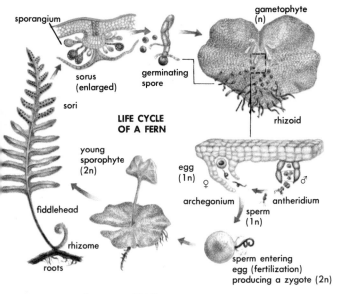

sporangium

sorus (enlarged)

sori

germinating spore

gametophyte (n)

rhizoid

LIFE CYCLE OF A FERN

young sporophyte (2n)

egg (1n) ♀

archegonium

antheridium ♂

sperm (1n)

fiddlehead

rhizome

roots

sperm entering egg (fertilization) producing a zygote (2n)

REPRODUCTION IN FERNS also involves two generations, but each grows independently. The conspicuous sporophyte has true roots, stems, and leaves. Spores develop by meiosis in sporangia, usually in clusters (sori) on the underside of the leaves. When mature, the sporangia break open and release the spores. Wind-carried spores that fall on damp soil may develop into flat, heart-shaped gametophytes.

On their underside the gametophytes produce eggs in archegonia and sperms in antheridia. Eggs and sperms on each plant usually mature at different times, assuring cross-fertilization. The resulting zygote has a diploid (2n) chromosome count and divides by mitosis to form an embryo that develops into the sporophyte fern. The gametophyte dies after the sporophyte has become established as an independent plant.

REPRODUCTION IN SEED PLANTS involves an alternation of generations, as does that of mosses and ferns (pp. 104–105). The sporophyte, with 2n chromosomes, is the large and independent plant. The gametophyte, microscopic and parasitic on the sporophyte, has the haploid (1n) chromosome number as a result of meiosis. In most gymnosperms, the gametophytes are borne on the cone scales, as shown in the life history of pines on p. 54.

Angiosperm gametophytes are produced in flowers, the most highly evolved structures for plant reproduction. The female gametophytes, or embryo sacs, form in the flower ovules; the male gametophytes form from the pollen grains produced in the anther. A pollen grain must be transferred to a flower's stigma for pollination to occur. Sperms develop in the pollen tube, and fertilization of the egg occurs in the embryo sac.

PARTS OF A COMPLETE FLOWER

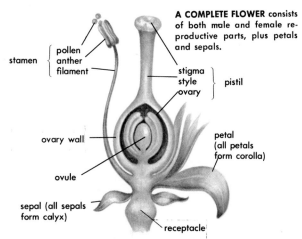

A COMPLETE FLOWER consists of both male and female reproductive parts, plus petals and sepals.

stamen { pollen / anther / filament }

stigma / style / ovary } pistil

ovary wall

ovule

petal (all petals form corolla)

sepal (all sepals form calyx)

receptacle

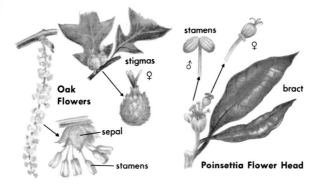

Oak Flowers

stigmas ♀

sepal

stamens

stamens ♂

♀

bract

Poinsettia Flower Head

INCOMPLETE FLOWERS

FLOWERS produce the seeds from which new plants grow. Many flowers are inconspicuous and are neither beautiful nor fragrant. Nor do all flowers consist of the same parts. A flower that lacks any of those parts shown on page 106 is incomplete.

A perfect flower has both types of reproductive structures, though it may lack other parts. The grass flower on p. 99 is a perfect flower that lacks petals and sepals. Flowers with only one type of

reproductive organ, as the oak flowers shown here, are imperfect. Those with only male reproductive organs are staminate; those with only female organs, pistillate. The small staminate and pistillate flowers of Poinsettia grow separately on the same flower head. Red leaflike bracts that grow below the flowers are commonly mistaken for petals.

Sunflowers have a floral head of complete flowers surrounded by incomplete "ray" flowers.

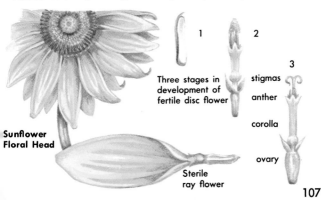

Sunflower Floral Head

1   2

Three stages in development of fertile disc flower

3

stigmas

anther

corolla

ovary

Sterile ray flower

107

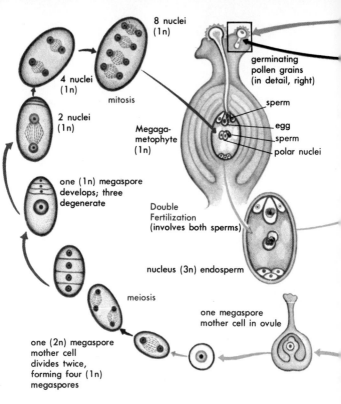

8 nuclei (1n)

4 nuclei (1n)

mitosis

2 nuclei (1n)

Megagametophyte (1n)

one (1n) megaspore develops; three degenerate

Double Fertilization (involves both sperms)

nucleus (3n) endosperm

meiosis

one (2n) megaspore mother cell divides twice, forming four (1n) megaspores

one megaspore mother cell in ovule

germinating pollen grains (in detail, right)

sperm
egg
sperm
polar nuclei

THE LIFE CYCLE of angiosperms differs from that of gymnosperms in the unique double fertilization that occurs in the gametophyte. True fertilization (fusion of the sperm and egg) is accompanied by another fusion process (that of a second sperm with the polar nuclei). This feature is shown in the diagram above, as are the meiotic divisions of the megaspore and microspore.

To trace the sequence of events in the diagram, start with the complete flower. Red arrows indicate the female gametophyte generation (1n); blue, the male (1n); and green, the sporophyte (2n), and the endosperm (3n).

In the ovule, meiotic divisions followed by mitotic divisions of the megaspore result in a (1n) megagametophyte containing eight nuclei. Of these, six develop cell

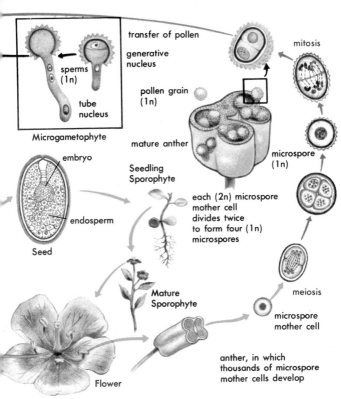

transfer of pollen

generative nucleus

sperms (1n)

tube nucleus

Microgametophyte

pollen grain (1n)

mature anther

mitosis

microspore (1n)

each (2n) microspore mother cell divides twice to form four (1n) microspores

embryo

endosperm

Seed

Seedling Sporophyte

Mature Sporophyte

meiosis

microspore mother cell

anther, in which thousands of microspore mother cells develop

Flower

walls, one of which becomes the egg cell. The two remaining are the polar nuclei.

Divisions that occur in the anther produce numerous pollen grains, each with two nuclei. When a pollen grain reaches a receptive stigma, it is held fast, germinates, and develops a tube that grows down through the style. Inside is a tube nucleus, plus two sperms that are formed by division of the generative nucleus. The tube enters the ovule, penetrates the megagametophyte, and releases the sperms. One of the sperms unites with the egg to form the zygote; the other unites with the two fused polar nuclei to form a 3n endosperm nucleus. The endosperm nucleus divides many times, becoming the food storing tissue for the developing embryo (p. 111).

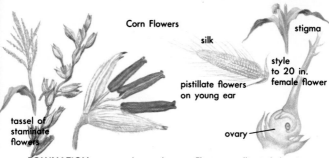

Corn Flowers

silk

stigma

style
to 20 in.
female flower

pistillate flowers
on young ear

tassel of
staminate
flowers

ovary

POLLINATION occurs when pollen is transferred from a stamen to a stigma. In self-pollination, the pollen is from the same flower or from another flower on the same plant. Self-pollination, which tends to limit genetic variation, is prevented in many plants by differences in rate of maturation of stamens and pistils.

In cross-pollination, pollen is transferred to a flower on another plant of the same species by wind, insects, or other means. Wind-pollinated flowers are usually small and not showy. In corn (above), the pistillate flowers form the ear. Staminate flowers form the tassel.

Flowers pollinated by insects typically have glands that secrete nectar and also have brightly colored petals or bracts. Some have special devices that aid insect pollination. In Salvia (below), the pressure of a bee pushing against the back of the flower causes the anthers to dip down. Pollen is brushed off on the bee's back, and when it visits an older flower on which the stigmas have matured and are receptive, the pollen is picked up by them. Cross-pollination is enforced when staminate and pistillate flowers occur on separate plants, as in the case of hollies and willows.

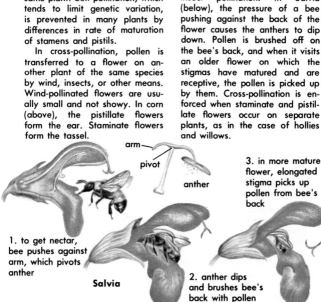

arm

pivot

anther

1. to get nectar, bee pushes against arm, which pivots anther

Salvia

2. anther dips and brushes bee's back with pollen

3. in more mature flower, elongated stigma picks up pollen from bee's back

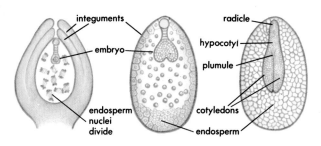

labels: integuments, embryo, endosperm nuclei divide, radicle, hypocotyl, plumule, cotyledons, endosperm

EMBRYO AND SEED DEVELOPMENT begins with the first division of the zygote. While the young embryo develops, the endosperm nucleus divides many times. Cell walls eventually form between the many endosperm nuclei, making the multicellular endosperm tissue that furnishes food for the embryo.

The fully developed embryo consists of a radicle (embryonic root), which develops into the primary root; the hypocotyl; one or two cotyledons; and a plumule, or epicotyl (the first bud). The protective seed coat forms from the outer layers, the integuments of the ovule.

SEEDLING DEVELOPMENT starts when seeds are placed in a suitable environment, such as moist soil. Imbibition and osmosis (pp. 82–83) account for the intake of necessary water. Mitosis occurs in the plumule and the radicle, giving rise to a rapidly elongating embryo. The hypocotyl, just below the cotyledons, may increase in length rapidly also. In some seeds this is important as it quickly lifts the cotyledons and plumule above the soil. Photosynthesis starts in the cotyledons as soon as they turn green in the light. In other seeds the hypocotyl does not develop as extensively.

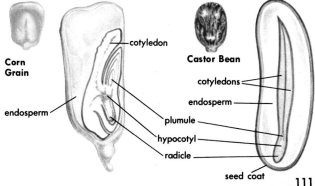

Corn Grain — cotyledon, endosperm

Castor Bean — cotyledons, endosperm, plumule, hypocotyl, radicle, seed coat

111

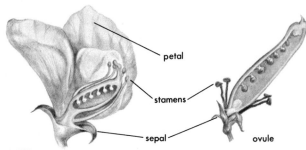

petal

stamens

sepal

ovule

ovary
(superior: above
other floral
parts)

THE PEA POD—A DRY FRUIT

FRUITS develop from ovaries, and seeds develop from the fertilized ovules. A fruit may develop from one or more mature ovaries and include any other structures that ripen with it (pistil, and in some cases the receptacle and other floral organs). The ovary wall of the ripe fruit is called the pericarp and may consist of two or three distinct layers. The pericarp may vary; it may be soft or hard, dry or fleshy.

IN THE PEA (above), the ovary wall forms a dry pod that splits when ripe and releases the seeds. Other dry fruits, such as grains and nuts, usually contain only one or few seeds and do not open.

THE APPLE (below) is called an accessory fruit because most of the edible portion develops from the floral tube. The seeds and the surrounding ovary wall form the core of the apple.

APPLE—A FLESHY ACCESSORY

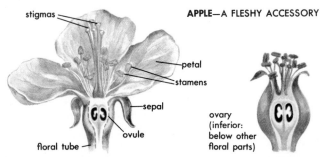

stigmas

petal

stamens

sepal

ovule

floral tube

ovary
(inferior:
below other
floral parts)

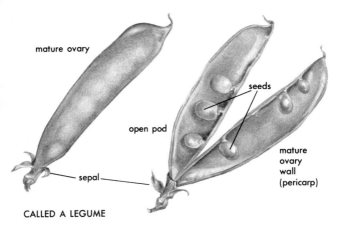

mature ovary

seeds

open pod

mature ovary wall (pericarp)

sepal

CALLED A LEGUME

FRUIT DEVELOPMENT usually does not begin until the egg is fertilized; however, both pollen-growth hormones and synthetic growth substances can stimulate the development of an ovary without fertilization. In such cases, the fruit develops; the seeds do not. Navel oranges, bananas, pineapples, and some grapes are fruits that regularly develop without the usual necessity of seed formation.

BOTANICALLY, a "fruit" is clearly distinguished from the common concept of its being only a soft, sweet, edible plant part. Many so-called vegetables (the word vegetable is not a botanical term) are fruits—string beans, tomatoes, squash, peppers, cucumbers, and others. The form, texture, and structure of fruits vary. Various types and their classification are shown on pages 114–115.

FRUIT CALLED A POME

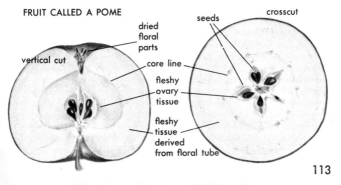

crosscut

seeds

dried floral parts

vertical cut

core line

fleshy ovary tissue

fleshy tissue derived from floral tube

113

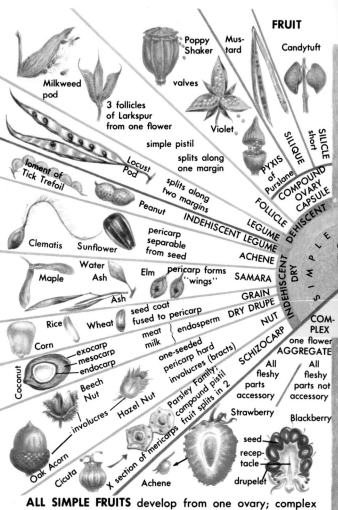

FRUIT

Poppy Shaker

Mus-tard

Candytuft

Milkweed pod

valves

3 follicles of Larkspur from one flower

Violet

SILIQUE

SILICLE short

simple pistil

splits along one margin

PYXIS of Purslane

Locust Pod

loment of Tick Trefoil

splits along two margins

COMPOUND OVARY CAPSULE

FOLLICLE

Peanut

LEGUME

DEHISCENT

INDEHISCENT LEGUME

Clematis

Sunflower

pericarp separable from seed

ACHENE

Maple

Water Ash

Elm

pericarp forms "wings"

SAMARA

Ash

GRAIN

Rice

Wheat

seed coat fused to pericarp

DRY DRUPE

DRY

INDEHISCENT

S I M P L E

Corn

meat | milk } endosperm

one-seeded pericarp hard involucres (bracts)

NUT

SCHIZOCARP

COM-PLEX

one flower
AGGREGATE

Coconut

exocarp
mesocarp
endocarp

Beech Nut

Hazel Nut

Parsley Family; compound pistil fruit splits in 2

All fleshy parts accessory

All fleshy parts not accessory

involucres

Strawberry

Blackberry

Oak Acorn

Cicuta

X section of mericarps

Achene

seed
recep-tacle
drupelet

ALL SIMPLE FRUITS develop from one ovary; complex fruits develop from more than one. By starting at the center and reading outward in the chart, many common

114

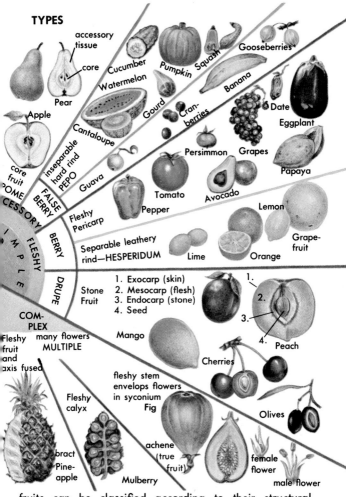

TYPES

accessory tissue

core

Pear

Apple

core fruit

POME

ACCESSORY

SIMPLE

FLESHY

Cucumber

Watermelon

Cantaloupe

Gourd

Pumpkin

Squash

Banana

Gooseberries

Cranberries

Date

Eggplant

inseparable hard rind PEPO

FALSE BERRY

Guava

Persimmon

Grapes

Papaya

Tomato

Avocado

Pepper

Fleshy Pericarp

BERRY

Lemon

Grapefruit

Separable leathery rind—HESPERIDUM

Lime

Orange

DRUPE

Stone Fruit

1. Exocarp (skin)
2. Mesocarp (flesh)
3. Endocarp (stone)
4. Seed

1.
2.
3.
4. Peach

COMPLEX

Fleshy fruit and axis fused

many flowers **MULTIPLE**

Mango

Cherries

fleshy stem envelops flowers in syconium **Fig**

Olives

Fleshy calyx

achene (true fruit)

female flower

male flower

bract Pineapple

Mulberry

fruits can be classified according to their structural characteristics. Dehiscent fruits open by splitting or other means when ripe. Indehiscent fruits do not.

VEGETATIVE PROPAGATION is a form of asexual reproduction that occurs normally in many plants. It is also used commercially to get fruit and crop plants to their yield stage rapidly and to develop large populations of plants that will produce identical fruits. Seedless fruits can be propagated only vegetatively.

Sweet Potato

suckers at base of Apple Tree

Iris rhizomes

Strawberry plants from stolons

Kalanchoe

ROOTS of some plants will produce buds and stems, and grow into new plants. Sweet potatoes and dahlias are familiar plants grown in this manner. Roots of other plants, such as apples, produce "suckers" that can be removed and planted. Root cuttings can be used to start such plants as camphor, locust, cherries, plums, and blackberries.

STEMS may also reproduce vegetatively, and cuttings are used to start many plants. The cut may be treated with a plant hormone (p. 90) to stimulate rooting. Rhizomes are underground stems that spread and produce new plants, as in irises. Irish potato tubers are produced on rhizomes.

Corms, such as those of gladioli and crocuses, are reproductive stems in which food is stored. Bulbs, in contrast, consist of storage leaves that surround a thickened stem.

Stolons, or runners, are stems that grow along the surface and produce stem buds at intervals, as in strawberries.

LEAVES of a few kinds of plants produce buds from which new plants grow, as in Kalanchoe. Begonias and African Violets can be and usually are propagated by leaf cuttings.

GRAFTING is used either to propagate hybrid plants because they do not breed true or to grow desirable varieties on sturdier or disease-resistant rootstocks. In all grafting, the cambium of the desired top (scion) must be placed in contact with the cambium of the root-stock (root system). New cambium, xylem, and phloem will then grow and connect identical tissues of the scion and stock.

Grafting is successful only if tissue compatibility exists between the scion and the rootstock. This generally restricts the choice of scion and rootstock to varieties of one species or to species of the same genus. Delicious and Jonathan are compatible cultivars of apples. Peaches will graft on certain plums, almonds, and cherries, since all are species in the same genus.

SCIONS may be single lateral buds or short lengths of stem with several buds. When single buds are used, the technique is called budding. Plastic wrapping and grafting wax are used to prevent drying of the scion before the cambiums unite.

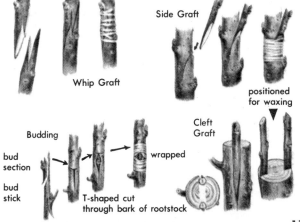

Side Graft

Whip Graft

positioned
for waxing

Budding

Cleft
Graft

bud
section

bud
stick

T-shaped cut
through bark of rootstock

wrapped

Every plant produced by sexual reproduction resembles its parents basically. Yet, no two individuals are exactly alike. However, both the similarities and the variations are due to heredity. Even when hereditary make-up is very similar, environment may still cause differences in appearance and behavior. Differences that are brought about by environment are not inherited.

Genetics is the study of how characteristics are inherited. Studies range from observing visible features to the chemistry of chromosomes, which are the carriers of hereditary traits. Sexual reproduction, in which there is a mixing of genetic materials from two parents, is the greatest source of variation. In asexual reproduction, variations occur only through mutations (p. 126).

SOME GENETIC

not paired 2n

2n paired

1n

CHROMOSOMES are nuclear structures that bear hereditary factors. Each species has a specific number of chromosomes, which can be seen and, counted during mitosis and meiosis (pp. 101 and 103). Chromosomes are formed of two equal longitudinal halves, or chromatids, visible under high magnification. Bits of chromosomes consisting mainly of DNA (p. 129) form genes that bear the hereditary factors.

DIPLOID NUCLEI contain two sets of paired chromosomes (2n), formed when the sex cells unite. Each chromosome in a pair bears factors for the same traits.

HAPLOID NUCLEI have only a single set of chromosomes (1n). This condition is characteristic of sex cells and arises during meiosis (p. 103).

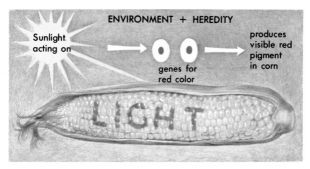

ENVIRONMENT + HEREDITY

Sunlight acting on → genes for red color → produces visible red pigment in corn

THE INTERACTION of heredity and environment determines the expression of a genetic characteristic. For instance, sun-red corn normally has yellow kernels but develops a red pigment when the kernels are exposed to sunlight.

All of the kernels on the ear above have a similar heredity, but portions of the husk were cut away to spell the word LIGHT. The kernels exposed to the light turned red, demonstrating the effects of environmental factors.

CONCEPTS

LINKAGE refers to the position, or order, of genes on a chromosome that results in groups of genes functioning as a unit. The genes for color and shape of seeds, for example, may be on the same chromosome, and thus are inherited together due to linkage. Genes influencing flower color, however, may be on chromosomes other than those for color and shape of seeds. Seed and flower traits are assorted and inherited independently.

DOMINANT TRAITS are those most commonly seen in a population; those seen less frequently are usually recessives. If two genes for a particular trait are unlike, they are heterozygous; if alike, homozygous. In the diagram, YY represents homozygous yellow; yy, homozygous green. Yy is heterozygous, but appears yellow because the yellow color is dominant over green.

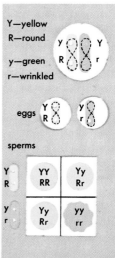

Y—yellow
R—round
y—green
r—wrinkled

eggs

sperms

	Y R	y r
Y R	YY RR	Yy Rr
y r	Yy Rr	yy rr

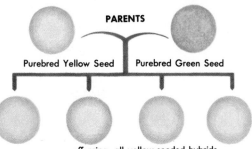

PARENTS

Purebred Yellow Seed   Purebred Green Seed

offspring: all yellow-seeded hybrids

MENDELIAN GENETICS began with Gregor Mendel's experiments in plant breeding about 1860. Plant breeders before him had assumed that a plant's appearance indicated its genetic makeup and that if it were crossed with a plant like itself the offspring would look the same. They assumed, for example, that yellow-seeded garden peas could produce only yellow-seeded offspring.

When Mendel crossed a yellow-seeded pea plant with one bearing green seeds (above), all of the offspring were yellow-seeded. Further, when these offspring were mated (below), both yellow- and green-seeded offspring occurred in the ratio of three yellows to one green. This showed that some traits in the genetic make-up of a plant may be hidden, or recessive.

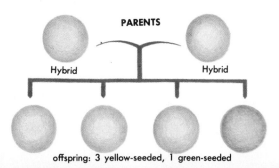

PARENTS

Hybrid   Hybrid

offspring: 3 yellow-seeded, 1 green-seeded

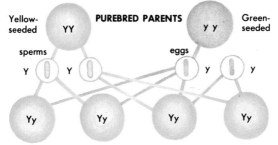

Yellow-seeded | **PUREBRED PARENTS** | Green-seeded

YY   yy

sperms   eggs

Y   Y   y   y

Yy   Yy   Yy   Yy

offspring: all heterozygous yellow

GENES, the determiners of inherited traits, are the complex bits of chromatin that occur along the chromosomes. For every trait or characteristic, a plant usually receives two genes—one from each parent. When sperms and eggs are produced, these paired genes separate so that each sperm or egg receives only one of the genes from each pair.

For example, a pea plant that is purebred for yellow seeds has two genes for yellow color, one on each of the paired or homologous chromosomes. This is shown above as YY. When a purebred yellow-seeded pea plant is crossed with a purebred green-seeded plant, shown above as yy, the offspring are genetically mixed or heterozygous, indicated as Yy.

The heterozygous seeds produced in such a cross appear yellow because the yellow is dominant whenever present. Green is recessive and shows only when both genes are for green color.

Crossing two heterozygous yellow-seeded offspring (Yy and Yy, below) provides proof that the green gene is present but masked. Three offspring are yellow-seeded —one is YY, two Yy. The fourth is a green-seeded homozygous recessive, yy. These ratios are seen only by examining individuals from numerous crosses.

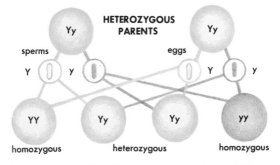

HETEROZYGOUS PARENTS

Yy   Yy

sperms   eggs

Y   y   Y   y

YY   Yy   Yy   yy

homozygous   heterozygous   homozygous

GENE COMBINATIONS may occur in such a great range of possibilities as to be almost unbelievable. A simple cross of two pairs of hybrid genes may produce 16 variations, as shown in the chart. A trihybrid cross (three traits, as for seed shape, color, and size) can produce 64 gene combinations in the second generation. Four traits may result in 256 different combinations. Every additional pair of genes multiplies the number of possible gene combinations in the offspring by four.

Each plant contains thousands of genes, hence the total number of combinations possible in the fertilized egg runs into the millions. Each plant is thus unquestionably unique in its genetic make-up, and observable variations occur with regularity.

A DIHYBRID CROSS ▶

For yellow and green color and for round and wrinkled shape.
Yellow and round are dominant traits.

A DIHYBRID CROSS, as charted, shows the genetic composition of each possible combination of sperm and egg. The four possible chromosome combinations in the sperm are shown across the top of the chart, and the four possible kinds of eggs along the left side. The checkerboard is then filled out by combining each kind of sperm with each kind of egg.

In genetic make-up, the kinds of offspring possible from such a cross are: yellow-round, yellow-wrinkled, green-round, and green-wrinkled, in a theoretical ratio of 9:3:3:1. Actually a very large population, or field sample, is needed in order to reach such a ratio in nature.

In practical genetics, the checkerboard method, with a few traits, can be used to work out the genetic make-up of either the offspring or the parents. If enough offspring are examined to have a sampling of all the various genetic types that might be expressed, these can be plotted on the checkerboard. Then the actual gene composition of the two parents can be determined.

Knowledge of genetic background is commonly used in plant breeding to develop breeding stock with such desirable features as resistance to disease and greater productivity. In flowers and shrubs, a more desirable appearance may be the purpose.

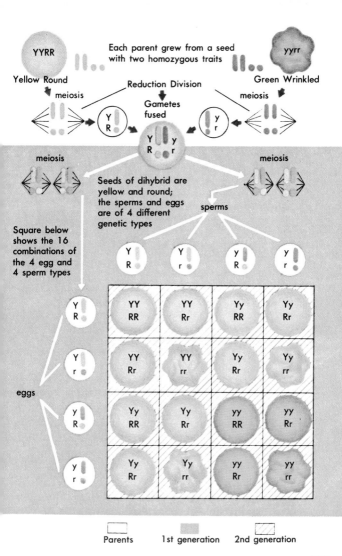

YYRR
Yellow Round

Each parent grew from a seed with two homozygous traits

yyrr
Green Wrinkled

meiosis

Reduction Division

meiosis

Gametes fused

Y
R

y
r

Y y
R r

meiosis

meiosis

Seeds of dihybrid are yellow and round; the sperms and eggs are of 4 different genetic types

sperms

Square below shows the 16 combinations of the 4 egg and 4 sperm types

	Y R	Y r	y R	y r
Y R	YY RR	YY Rr	Yy RR	Yy Rr
Y r	YY Rr	YY rr	Yy Rr	Yy rr
y R	Yy RR	Yy Rr	yy RR	yy Rr
y r	Yy Rr	Yy rr	yy Rr	yy rr

eggs

Parents   1st generation   2nd generation

123

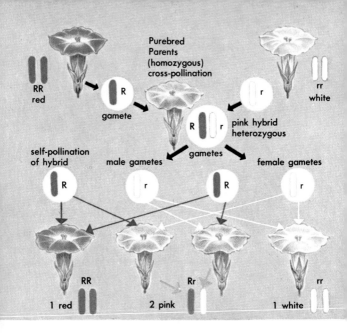

INCOMPLETE DOMINANCE sometimes occurs when the two genes of a pair seem equally effective in their influence on a trait. If purebred red-flowered four-o'-clocks (RR) are crossed with purebred white-flowered plants (rr), the offspring are all heterozygous (Rr) but have pink flowers. When these pink-flowered plants are crossed, their offspring appear in the ratio of one red, two pink, and one white.

Dominance may also be affected in some plants by the environment. Temperature, intensity of light, and other external factors may cause a change in the expected results. Chinese primroses grown at 68°F., for example, will produce red flowers, but if the plants are grown at 80°F., they produce white flowers.

OTHER COMPLEXITIES OF INHERITANCE

CROSSING OVER may occur in meiosis. When the chromosomes pair and twist together, they may break apart in such a way that an exchange of chromatin has occurred at their points of contact. This changes the original order (linkage) of the genes, and new hereditary combinations arise.

DELETIONS occur when small bits of a single chromosome break off. They may be lost, and the genes carried on that portion of the chromosome do not appear in the daughter nuclei. Or they may become attached to another chromosome (translocated) and thus alter the inheritance pattern.

INVERSIONS occur when a single chromosome breaks and then recombines itself in such a way that the original order of the genes is altered. No genes are lost in an inversion, but the complicating factor of their new position may affect the inheritance pattern.

MULTIPLE GENE INHERITANCE results from interaction of several incompletely dominant genes. Their cumulative effect may cause a variation in a trait or character. In wheat, for example, four genes influence grain color. When red and white grain varieties are crossed and their medium-red offspring are interbred, the grain color in the next generation ranges from red to white.

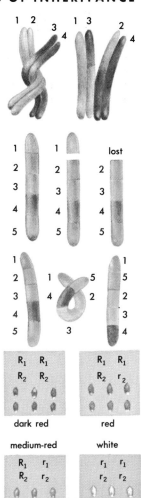

dark red

red

medium-red

white

MUTATIONS are abrupt inheritable changes brought about by alterations in a gene or a chromosome or by an increase in chromosome number. Plants showing these changes are called mutants. The rate of mutation occurrence can be increased artificially, but the results cannot be controlled. Navel oranges, nectarines, many varieties of potatoes, and variegated shrubs are mutants asexually propagated to retain desirable features.

Navel Orange   Nectarine   Loganberry

Euonymus

CHROMOSOME MUTATIONS include (1) changes in the normal number of chromosome sets, leading to a condition called polyploidy (p. 127), (2) loss of or addition of a chromosome or chromosome part; and (3) abnormal fusions during crossing over. Gene mutations are changes in single genes. Usually recessive, they may be unexpressed for generations.

Mutations are produced by internal disorders, such as inaccurate gene duplication, and by natural external forces, such as severe temperature changes and radiations. They are induced experimentally by use of atomic radiation, X-rays, chemicals, and sudden temperature changes. In laboratories, plants are bombarded with gamma or X-ray radiation to produce mutations. Researchers check the results for new types of plants with desirable features. Tens of thousands of plants may be treated before a desirable trait is obtained.

Changes due to atomic radiation

Snapdragon

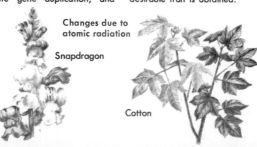

Cotton

| colchicine destroys spindle fibers during meiotic division | division stops and nuclear membrane forms around diploid nucleus | effects of colchicine wear off and spindle forms | chromosomes split and separate; diploid gametes form |

POLYPLOIDY refers to the number of chromosome sets in a cell. Haploid (1n) is one set; diploid (2n), two sets. A polyploid is any number more than the diploid. A sex cell (gamete) is normally haploid, but if a cell wall fails to form during meiosis, sex cells develop with two sets of chromosomes (diploid, or 2n). If one of these 2n sex cells is fertilized by a 1n sex cell, a triploid (3n) plant is produced. If two diploid sex cells unite, a tetraploid (4n) plant results. Polyploidy may occur naturally or may be induced by use of colchicine, as shown above.

Polyploid plants are usually more vigorous than diploids, but some are sterile. Seedless watermelons, Baldwin apples, Pink Beauty tulips, and Japanese flowering cherries are triploids. Most cultivated irises and many lilies are tetraploids.

TETRAPLOID LILY

DIPLOID LILY

INBREEDING (self-pollinating) results finally in a homozygous population. This establishes a line that tends to breed true, with both desirable and undesirable traits. For corn hybridization (below), inbred lines are selected to offset the undesirable recessive traits of one line with desirable dominant expressions of the same traits in another.

HYBRIDIZATION (cross-pollinating) of two inbred lines allows expression of the desirable dominant traits of both lines. This usually results also in "hybrid vigor"— plants more vigorous than those of either inbred line. Single-cross and double-cross hybrid corn developed in this manner always give greater yields than non-hybrid types. When the traits are segregated again in their offspring, this vigor may be lost. For this reason farmers plant hybrid corn seed produced under controlled conditions rather than seeds from their own crops.

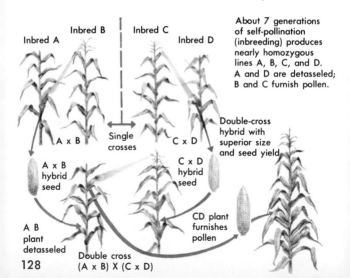

Inbred A

Inbred B

Inbred C

Inbred D

Single crosses

A x B

C x D

About 7 generations of self-pollination (inbreeding) produces nearly homozygous lines A, B, C, and D. A and D are detasseled; B and C furnish pollen.

A x B hybrid seed

C x D hybrid seed

Double-cross hybrid with superior size and seed yield

A B plant detasseled

Double cross (A x B) X (C x D)

CD plant furnishes pollen

MODERN GENETICS originated when chemical analysis revealed that chromosomes contain two classes of molecules: proteins and nucleic acids. The nucleic acids occur in the cell in two forms: ribose nucleic acid (RNA) and deoxyribonucleic acid (DNA). The inheritance message seems to be coded in the structure of DNA.

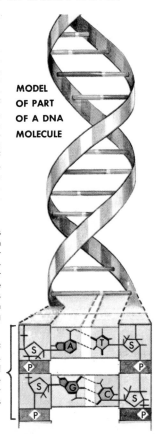

MODEL
OF PART
OF A DNA
MOLECULE

DNA is found mostly in the chromosomes of the nucleus. In structure it consists of two spiraling chains of sugar molecules alternating with phosphoric acid molecules. The sugar molecules of one chain are linked to the sugar molecules of the other chain by pairs of nitrogenous bases, of which there are four: thymine, guanine, cytosine, and adenine. Thus, the entire molecule is believed to look somewhat like a long, spiral ladder with pairs of nitrogenous bases forming the rungs. The important point is that each ''cross rung'' always consists of one of two pairs: cytosine-guanine or thymine-adenine.

A CHROMOSOME contains specific amounts of DNA with bases held together, one after the other, in many different sequences. Thus, genes are thought to be specific sequences of these units containing specific numbers of nitrogen bases. Gene function is largely that of programming protein production.

The basic unit of DNA consists of a nucleotide, consisting of phosphoric acid (P), sugar (S), and one nitrogenous base—guanine (G), cytosine (C), adenine (A), or thymine (T). Four nucleotides shown.

129

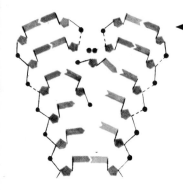

DUPLICATION, or replication, is the biologists' term for the way DNA makes copies of hereditary information, which is the basis by which organisms make copies of themselves. How the replication takes place is not fully known, but is sometimes described as the "zipper effect"—the separation of the two halves of the "spiral ladder" (as shown). Each half then supposedly attracts to itself the necessary substances to replace its separated partner to form a new helix.

RNA, while present in the chromosomes in small amounts, occurs principally outside the nucleus in the cytoplasm, although it is apparently made in the nucleus. RNA is very similar in molecular arrangement to DNA with three differences: First, the sugar molecule is ribose instead of deoxyribose. (The sugar in DNA has one less oxygen atom than that of RNA.) Second, uracil replaces thymine. Finally, most RNA contains many single-stranded sections instead of a double helical pattern.

Three kinds of RNA are known to exist: (1) ribosomal (r-RNA), (2) transfer (t-RNA), and (3) messenger (m-RNA). Each has its own function; but the main result is that RNA carries genetic information coded in DNA from the nucleus to protein building sites (ribosomes) in the cytoplasm surrounding the nucleus. The importance lies in the fact that a particular protein is always a part of a particular enzyme (the "one gene—one enzyme" concept). In turn, particular enzymes control specific processes.

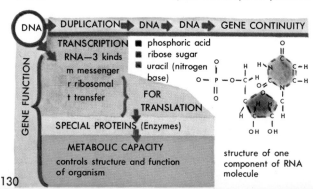

structure of one component of RNA molecule

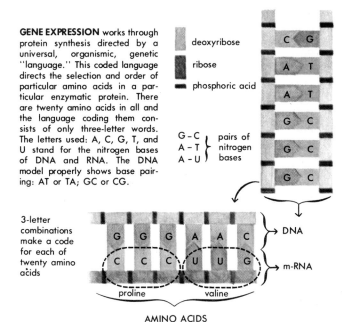

GENE EXPRESSION works through protein synthesis directed by a universal, organismic, genetic "language." This coded language directs the selection and order of particular amino acids in a particular enzymatic protein. There are twenty amino acids in all and the language coding them consists of only three-letter words. The letters used: A, C, G, T, and U stand for the nitrogen bases of DNA and RNA. The DNA model properly shows base pairing: AT or TA; GC or CG.

deoxyribose
ribose
phosphoric acid

G – C } pairs of
A – T } nitrogen
A – U } bases

3-letter combinations make a code for each of twenty amino acids

proline   valine

AMINO ACIDS

Double-stranded DNA (at right above) separates and the left strand codes RNA for two amino acids as shown.

IN TRANSLATION the m-RNA migrates from the nucleus and associates closely with a ribosome and its r-RNA. Transfer RNA locates its coded amino acid in the cytoplasm and joins it chemically. This t-RNA, linked with its amino acid, then migrates to the ribosome with the m-RNA. Here the same coding rules position the amino acid as regulated by the code on the m-RNA. Other t-RNA molecules bring their coded amino acid into position on the m-RNA at the ribosome. Finally, the entire code of the m-RNA is used and an enzyme protein is created. In this way, DNA with its genes operates through RNA to give genetic expression through enzyme control of essential life processes. In other words, what an organism is and what it does is the combined result of its metabolism and the effects of its environment. Modern genetics has become a combination of Mendelian and molecular concepts.

EVOLUTION

Evolution, the continual change of living things, is the result of variations transmitted by genetics and screened through time. Evidences of these changes are many. A historical record is provided by fossils. Changes are revealed also by comparisons of plant structures and by plant physiology. Further clues are found in plant distribution and geography, in biochemistry, and in genetic analysis.

EVOLUTION began to receive world-wide attention after Charles Darwin published *The Origin of Species by Means of Natural Selection*, in 1859.

Darwin noted that no two sexually produced individuals are exactly alike. A population of plants or animals produces more offspring than its environment can support. Only the best adapted survive, passing their characteristics to their young. This process of natural selection was the core of Darwin's theory. The mechanism of heredity was discovered later.

We know now that evolution is the result of both heredity and environment. A species that is better adapted to its environment as a result of a change in its genetic make-up survives (survival of fittest); a species that loses features fitting it to its environment may die out. A new species may appear suddenly as a result of a mutation. Isolation of breeding units prevents the exchange of genes in sexual reproduction and, as shown below, may also produce new species over a long period of time.

A population changes constantly due to the combined effects of environment and heredity. In A, the interchange of genes was complete.

In B a geographic barrier has interrupted this gene interchange. New species may develop from the isolated population.

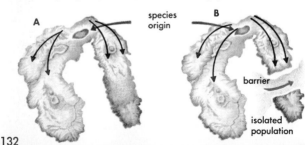

species origin

A

B

barrier

isolated population

FOSSILIZATION occurs when minerals replace original structures in such a way that even cell details are preserved. The famous petrified forest of Arizona is an excellent example. It consists largely of ancient members of a plant group (Araucaria), once world-wide, that now occurs only in a limited part of South America and in Australia. Sometimes fossilization involved mineralization that produced stones of gem quality.

petrifaction
showing wood detail

FOSSILS, which are preserved evidences of life of the past, provide one of the clearest proofs of evolution. Some are actual remains, though such preservations are rare. More commonly, fossils are impressions or replacements left in ancient muds or sands that later changed to rocks.

Evidences that life on earth has prevailed over 3 billion years is substantiated through analysis of radioactive minerals. The record reveals an increasing complexity in plants from the oldest to the youngest rocks.

fossil impression
in rock

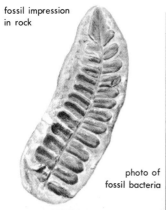

E. S. Barghoorn

photo of
fossil bacteria

ERA	PERIOD	EPOCH	TIME IN MILLIONS OF YEARS	MAJOR DEVELOPMENTS
CENOZOIC	Quaternary	Recent / Pleistocene	0	
CENOZOIC	Tertiary	Pliocene / Miocene / Oligocene / Eocene / Paleocene	63	short life cycle (annuals)
MESOZOIC	Cretaceous		135	special pollinating mechanisms / less woodiness
MESOZOIC	Jurassic		181	double fertilization / seeds in ovaries
MESOZOIC	Triassic		230	flowering habit
PALEOZOIC	Permian		280	seed-bearing cones / perennial habit
PALEOZOIC	Carboniferous — Pennsylvanian		310	woodiness: treelike / evergreen habit
PALEOZOIC	Carboniferous — Mississippian		345	seed-bearing ferns / life cycle dominated by sporophyte
PALEOZOIC	Devonian		405	development of stems, roots, and leaves
PALEOZOIC	Silurian		425	
PALEOZOIC	Ordovician		500	development of some tissues for growth on land / green algae and others with nuclei and plastids
PALEOZOIC	Cambrian			fungi and algae that reproduce sexually and also by mitosis / blue-green algae, capable of photosynthesis / chemosynthetic and photosynthetic bacteria
	Pre-Cambrian		600	single-celled organisms without nuclei, reproducing by fission

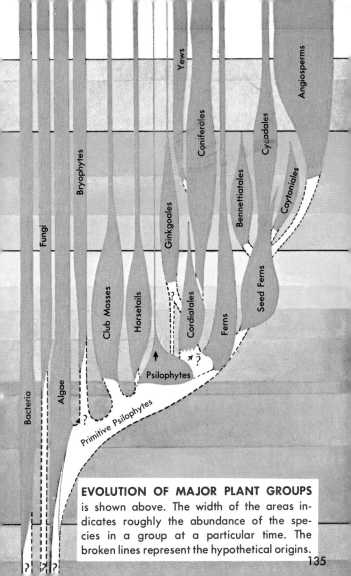

Bacteria

Fungi

Algae

Bryophytes

Club Mosses

Horsetails

Psilophytes

Primitive Psilophytes

Ginkgoales

Cordaitales

Ferns

Seed Ferns

Yews

Coniferales

Bennettitales

Cycadales

Caytoniales

Angiosperms

EVOLUTION OF MAJOR PLANT GROUPS is shown above. The width of the areas indicates roughly the abundance of the species in a group at a particular time. The broken lines represent the hypothetical origins.

EVOLUTION OF LAND PLANTS began in the Devonian Period some 400 million years ago (pp. 134–135). Land plants gradually developed vascular tissues in their stems, giving them support. Their flowers are specialized

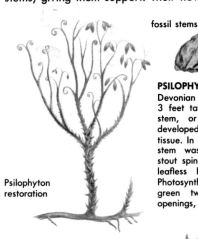

Psilophyton restoration

fossil stems

PSILOPHYTON, one of the Devonian land plants, grew about 3 feet tall from an underground stem, or rhizome, which had developed a simple vascular tissue. In some species, the aerial stem was covered with short, stout spines, and the tips of the leafless branches were coiled. Photosynthesis took place in the green twigs, which contained openings, or stomates.

LEPIDODENDRON, typical plants of warm Pennsylvanian swamps, formed much of our coal. More than 100 fossil species of these giant trees have been found in coal beds. Some grew 125 feet tall. The petioles of their narrow, five-foot leaves left spirals of diamond-shaped scars on the branches. Lepidodendron's few living relatives, the club mosses, are small.

fossil stem

Lepidodendron restoration

reproductive structures that insure sexual reproduction with a maximum exchange of genetic materials. Some significant plant fossils and restorations of the plant structures are shown here.

fossil trunk

Cycadeoidea restoration

CYCADS were typical of the kinds of gymnosperms common during the Jurassic. They bore flower-like reproductive structures on their bulbous trunk, from which grew frondlike leaves much like those of the modern Zamia. The closely related *Williamsonias*, resembling palms, grew as far north as Greenland. Present-day cycads consist of about 65 species that grow in the tropics or subtropics.

ANDROMEDA represents the flowering plants, or angiosperms, that arose during the Tertiary. Azaleas and rhododendrons are among its familiar modern relatives. The flower shown here is like those preserved in the fossil resin (amber) of conifers that also grew in those times. Many other families of plants common today became established during Tertiary times.

Andromeda restoration

fossil preserved in amber

137

RELIC PLANTS, or "living fossils," are rare species that are found also as fossils. These living links to the past provide important clues to ancient climates as well as to the geological age of groups of plants, for it is assumed that the plants persist today in areas where the climate has remained much the same as in their original range. Cycads (p. 137), for example, were once widespread. This indicates that the geographical areas where the fossils are found were tropical or subtropical when the plants grew there.

REDWOODS, among the largest and oldest of all living things, formerly grew as far eastward as New Jersey. It was especially abundant in central Colorado. Today, the Coast Redwood grows only in the "fog belt," a narrow strip along the California and Oregon coasts.

METASEQUOIA, or Dawn Redwood, once grew throughout the Northern Hemisphere, as far north as the Arctic Circle. As the climate cooled, the tree's range diminished. It was known only as a fossil until a living forest was found in a remote part of southwestern China in 1944.

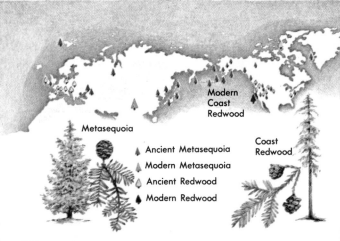

Modern Coast Redwood

Metasequoia

Coast Redwood

▲ Ancient Metasequoia
▲ Modern Metasequoia
◊ Ancient Redwood
◆ Modern Redwood

THE DIRECTION OF EVOLUTION is usually progressive—that is, from the simple to the more complex. Evolutionary trees (p. 137) illustrate this common path.

A species is generally suited for a specific set of environmental conditions. If the environment changes, a highly specialized type may not be able to adapt and will become extinct while a species following a simpler, more generalized direction continues to evolve. The reverse could also occur, however. Two common evolutionary directions are shown below.

Pinesap   Witchweed   Lovevine   Indian Pipe

RETROGRESSIVE evolution results in structurally simpler types from the more complex. All the plants above evolved from ancestors with chlorophyll. All now either have little or no chlorophyll. They exist as parasites or partial parasites.

PARALLEL evolution occurs when plants of different genera or even different families have evolved in similar directions. Often, as shown below, species of different families look so much alike they can be distinguished only by careful examination.

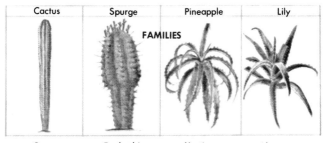

Cactus	Spurge	Pineapple	Lily

FAMILIES

Cereus   Euphorbia   Hectia   Aloe

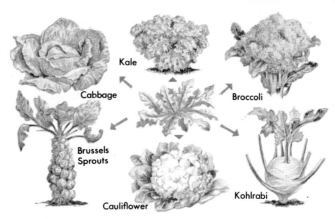

Kale

Cabbage

Broccoli

Brussels Sprouts

Kohlrabi

Cauliflower

DOMESTIC HYBRIDS sometimes result in new species, hence represent accelerated evolution. They may have little resemblance to their wild ancestors as shown in the cultivated varieties produced from wild cabbage. Evidence indicates, too, that hybrids occur regularly in nature. New species of weeds have appeared in areas where man has destroyed original biotic communities.

HYBRIDS are crosses between two species. Usually they are sterile diploids. Occasionally, however, the chromosome number is increased in faulty meiosis (p. 102–103). Most commonly a tetraploid (doubled chromosomes) is produced. Tetraploids are fertile, crossing freely with one an-

other and less so with their diploid ancestors. Thus they may produce new species rapidly, often within a few generations.

Scott's Spleenwort, a hybrid between Ebony Spleenwort and the Walking Fern, occurs naturally and can also be duplicated in controlled breeding.

Ebony Spleenwort

Scott's Spleenwort

Walking Fern

THE DEVELOPMENT OF CORN is another example of an evolutionary process in recent times. It may become to plant science what the story of the evolution of the horse is to animal science.

At least five types of corn are now recognized: pop (1), flint (5), flour (3, 4), dent (6), and sweet (2). The origin of these modern types of corn is not certain, though it is clear that they developed somewhere in the American tropics. Pollen grains estimated to be 80,000 years old have been found in layers 200 feet below ground at Mexico City. They have been identified as being from wild corn and suggest strongly that corn had a Mexican origin.

Teosinte and Tripsacum, two living wild relatives, have been hybridized with modern corn to obtain possible genetic evidence of corn's origin. Studies of accumulated trash in dry caves where man lived in prehistoric times have so far been most revealing, however. In the lowest, hence oldest layer of the floor in a cave in Mexico, tiny ears of corn less than an inch long have been found. This corn, which dates to about 5000 B.C., is probably much like the original wild corn from which man developed the five modern types. This primitive corn is now extinct.

In shallower, more recent layers of the cave a fairly sequential record of corn development is found. Some of the fossil specimens found there resemble the corn that is grown today in some of the warm regions of North and South America.

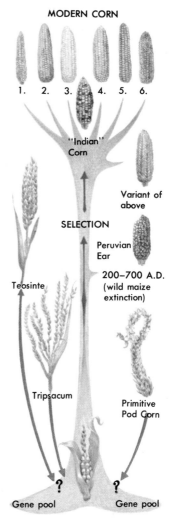

MODERN CORN

1.   2.   3.   4.   5.   6.

"Indian" Corn

Variant of above

SELECTION

Peruvian Ear

200–700 A.D. (wild maize extinction)

Teosinte

Tripsacum

Primitive Pod Corn

? Gene pool   ? Gene pool

WILD MAIZE

141

PLANTS AND THEIR ENVIRONMENT

Natural communities are formed of plants and animals that depend on the same environment and on each other for raw materials and food from which they derive energy. Each natural community, or ecosystem, has a well-organized structure and appears to be stable. Studies reveal, however, that communities change constantly. These changes, whether large or small, are usually measurable only over a long period of time. Often one change triggers another and thus creates a chain reaction. In time, a total plant population changes.

PHYSICAL FACTORS determining the kinds of plants in a community are mainly climate and soil. Temperature, light, and precipitation are the principal climatic factors. Some plants, for example, grow only in hot deserts; others, in cool bogs. Some can tolerate varied conditions.

Soils are the source of moisture and minerals. Soil texture affects the amount of oxygen available for seed germination, root growth, and bacterial action.

Physical factors may be localized. A windbreak protects plants from winds and also reduces loss of water by transpiration.

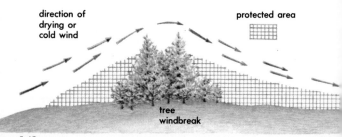

direction of drying or cold wind

protected area

tree windbreak

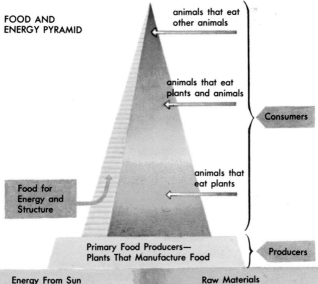

FOOD AND ENERGY PYRAMID

animals that eat other animals

animals that eat plants and animals

Consumers

animals that eat plants

Food for Energy and Structure

Primary Food Producers— Plants That Manufacture Food

Producers

Energy From Sun

Raw Materials

BIOLOGICAL FACTORS are complex, including interdependencies of organisms that are food producers, or storers, and food consumers, or users. In nature, these factors working together bring about a balanced condition that tends to perpetuate the system yet allowing for slow change.

At each step in a food chain the number of consumer organisms and the available energy decreases; the size of the individuals increases. This concept is illustrated by the pyramid above.

The three-step food chain below is one of the simplest. Most food chains involve many steps and overlap other food chains.

1,000 lbs. of phytoplankton ➡ 100 lbs. of krill ➡ 1 lb. of whale

Three-Step Food Chain

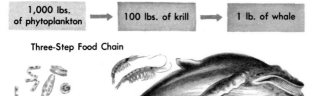

143

CYCLES of materials and energy are necessary to support life. In the process there is a recycling of material derived from both living and dead organisms. Microorganisms play an important role in these cycles, which vary from one habitat to another. Some important examples are given here.

CARBON is found in all organic compounds. In the form of carbon dioxide it is utilized with water in photosynthesis of basic foods by plants. In this process, oxygen is released into the atmosphere. This is virtually the only means of oxygen replenishment to the atmosphere. Both plants and animals release carbon dioxide in respiration returning it to the inorganic realm of water and air. Carbon in the plant and animal tissues is also returned to the cycle by decay. Thus, the same carbon atoms are used over and over. Sometimes, as in coal and limestone, the carbon atoms may be out of circulation for long periods. Today, pollution is a major concern as it favors locking carbon into CO_2.

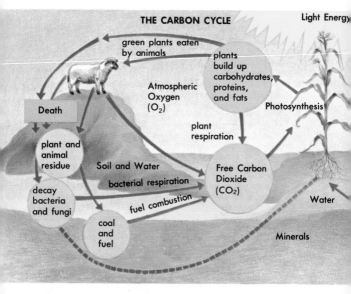

THE CARBON CYCLE

Light Energy

green plants eaten by animals

plants build up carbohydrates, proteins, and fats

Atmospheric Oxygen (O_2)

Photosynthesis

Death

plant respiration

plant and animal residue

Soil and Water

bacterial respiration

Free Carbon Dioxide (CO_2)

Water

decay bacteria and fungi

fuel combustion

coal and fuel

Minerals

NITROGEN is as essential to life as is carbon. It is a part of all amino acids and proteins. From the air it cannot be used directly by animals or by most plants. Some kinds of bacteria, however, can convert atmospheric nitrogen into usable organic compounds. Some of these bacteria live in the root nodules of legumes, such as clover. The nitrogen compounds they form are eventually released in decay and related processes as ammonia, then nitrites and nitrates. The ammonia and nitrates are absorbed by roots of plants and utilized in building proteins. Animals that eat these plants then convert the compounds into animal proteins.

WATER is another essential material that is incorporated in all life forms. Though its distribution is not uniform, the supply of water on earth is adequate and is reusable. It is circulated from the atmosphere to land and water—then back into the atmosphere. Mineral salts are circulated in solution in water.

Plants return much water to the atmosphere by transpiration (p. 83). They also intercept rainfall, thus aiding in its immediate evaporation. On the other hand, the shade afforded by plants and thick layers of dead leaves on the soil cools the soil, slows down evaporation, and increases water-holding capacity of soil.

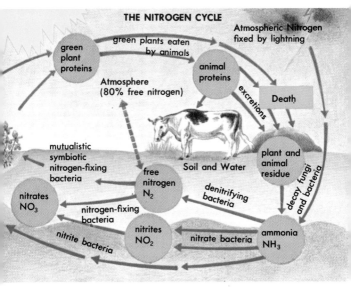

THE NITROGEN CYCLE

Atmospheric Nitrogen fixed by lightning

green plant proteins

green plants eaten by animals

animal proteins

Atmosphere (80% free nitrogen)

excretions

Death

mutualistic symbiotic nitrogen-fixing bacteria

free nitrogen N₂

Soil and Water

plant and animal residue

nitrates NO₃

nitrogen-fixing bacteria

denitrifying bacteria

decay fungi and bacteria

nitrite bacteria

nitrites NO₂

nitrate bacteria

ammonia NH₃

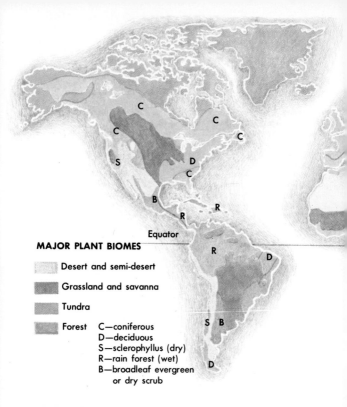

MAJOR PLANT BIOMES

Forest
- C—coniferous
- D—deciduous
- S—sclerophyllus (dry)
- R—rain forest (wet)
- B—broadleaf evergreen or dry scrub

Desert and semi-desert

Grassland and savanna

Tundra

Equator

BIOMES is the term used by ecologists to define the largest plant communities, covering broad areas of the earth. They establish the character of a region—as, for example, the tropical rain forests along the equator and the extensive coniferous forests of the North. Biomes consist of many smaller associations of plants that are generally named for the dominant plants in them. Thus, oak-hickory and beech-maple forests are associations in deciduous forests. Man's settlements and agriculture have altered all biomes.

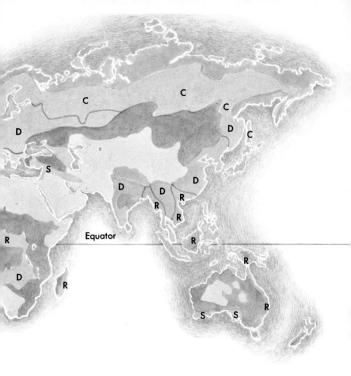

Equator

THE MAP above shows the distribution of major plant biomes that require about the same type of environment. The adaptability of plants to their environment leads to similarities of form in plants on different continents, though the plants may be of different species or families. For example, succulent cacti of American deserts look very much like the succulent spurges that grow in the deserts of southern Africa (p. 139).

Plants grow also in such hostile environments as Greenland and Antarctica (not shown on the map). Their very presence in such environments demonstrates the great adaptability of living things. Both areas are cold deserts, with perpetual ice and snow. In Antarctica, three species of flowering plants, some mosses and liverworts, and numerous lichens thrive on the rocky outcroppings. Greenland has vegetation only along its southern edge.

PLANT SUCCESSION involves the orderly, progressive changes as one type of plant community gradually replaces another. Generally it is the dominant species in each stage that alters the environment in a way that ushers in the next stage. In some cases, the plants and animals that make up each succession stage and the duration of each stage can be predicted. The eventual result of succession is the climax stage, a balanced or stable community that tends to remain the same unless the environment is disturbed. The total of all the plants and animals, or biomass, also increases as a state of equilibrium is approached.

Most successions are slow, requiring many years to move from one stage to the next until the climax stage is reached. One of the fastest (shown at right) is the "old field succession" that occurs in abandoned cotton fields near pine forests in southeastern United States. The succession that occurs in a shallow pond may be even faster, depending on the original size and depth of the pond, the type of surrounding land, and the length of the growing season. Ponds in flat country usually fill up more slowly than do those in hilly areas.

POND SUCCESSION is an example of a community succession. The change from an aquatic to a dry-land community is often rapid, sometimes completed during a man's lifetime. As shown here, a new pond in a temperate region gradually fills with deposits (silt and soil) that wash in from the surrounding area or build up from the dead remains of plants and animals that live in the water or nearby. The pond becomes shallower.

As the water becomes too shallow for the plants of one stage, new kinds of vegetation appear. The amount of open water at the center continues to decrease as the lake fills in from the edges.

Common plants of the floating stage are water lilies and pondweeds. Swamp-stage plants are cattails, bullrushes, and arrowheads. At the climax stage, a forest may grow where once there was pond water. A climax community usually persists.

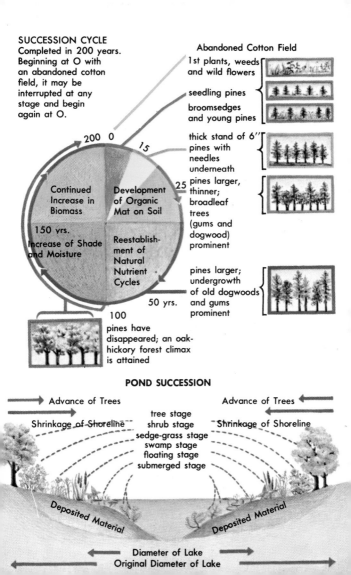

SUCCESSION CYCLE
Completed in 200 years. Beginning at O with an abandoned cotton field, it may be interrupted at any stage and begin again at O.

Abandoned Cotton Field

1st plants, weeds and wild flowers

seedling pines

broomsedges and young pines

thick stand of 6" pines with needles underneath

pines larger, thinner; broadleaf trees (gums and dogwood) prominent

pines larger; undergrowth of old dogwoods and gums prominent

pines have disappeared; an oak-hickory forest climax is attained

200 0
15
25
50 yrs.
100
150 yrs.

Continued Increase in Biomass

Development of Organic Mat on Soil

Increase of Shade and Moisture

Reestablishment of Natural Nutrient Cycles

POND SUCCESSION

Advance of Trees

Shrinkage of Shoreline

tree stage
shrub stage
sedge-grass stage
swamp stage
floating stage
submerged stage

Advance of Trees

Shrinkage of Shoreline

Deposited Material

Deposited Material

Diameter of Lake
Original Diameter of Lake

CLIMAX COMMUNITIES occur when the plant population of an area appears to be stable, or at equilibrium with the environment. Plants that die are then replaced by more of the same species. Depending on the climate and soil, a climax may be a forest, grassland, or desert.

In the same geographical region, a different number of succession stages may be required to reach the same climax stage, as shown below. A change in the soil or the climate may also interrupt the succession pattern and direct it to a different climax.

BEECH-MAPLE climax forests, typical of northeastern United States, may be reached on either rock or sand areas.

More steps and more time are required in reaching the climax on the rock site. Acids from early-stage or pioneer plants must start breaking down the rocks. Roots then grow into small cracks and wedge the rock apart. Debris and moisture accumulate, forming soil in which other species of plants can grow. Succession is faster in the finely divided sand.

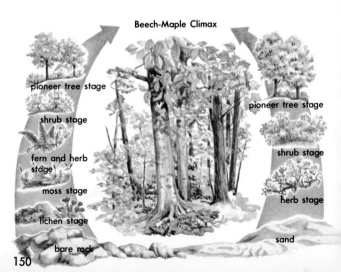

Beech-Maple Climax

pioneer tree stage

shrub stage

fern and herb stage

moss stage

lichen stage

bare rock

pioneer tree stage

shrub stage

herb stage

sand

TROPICAL RAIN FORESTS occur where the annual rainfall is 100 or more inches, the temperature from 65 to 95 degrees F. Broad-leaved evergreens produce forests of huge trees, their crowns forming a dense canopy. The dense shade restricts low-growing plants, but epiphytes and woody vines are abundant in the canopy. The fragile balance in these forests is easily disturbed. Recovery, if it occurs, is very slow. It may never occur. This type forest is least understood.

MONTANE CONIFEROUS FORESTS are belts of trees on the sides of mountains. Latitude, moisture, temperature, and slope all play a part in their pattern. In Arizona mountains, for example, the climax types change from desert at the mountain base to pinyon pines and junipers, then to Ponderosa Pines as moisture increases and the temperature becomes lower with increase in elevation. Above the pines are Douglas-firs, and finally, a spruce-fir community at the timberline.

DESERT COMMUNITIES exist as climax types where rainfall is less than 10 inches per year. Deserts may be either hot or cold. Their plants consist of four types: (1) xerophytes, with extensive but shallow root systems, reduced leaves, and thick cuticles; (2) annuals that can sprout, flower, and produce seeds within a few weeks; (3) phreatophytes, with deep root systems that penetrate to the water table; and (4) succulents, fleshy plants that absorb and store moisture.

MICROECOLOGY deals with the small but very significant environmental differences that occur in every plant community. Not uncommonly, for example, a temperature variation as great as 15 degrees F. occurs between the soil surface and a few feet above. So a small amount of soil or water may be the controlling factor that permits or restricts the growth of some kinds of plants.

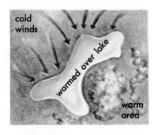

BODIES OF WATER influence the plants growing nearby. Along the shore, the relative humidity is higher and the light at ground level more intense than only a short distance into the surrounding vegetation. Shores on the downwind side are slightly warmer in winter, so killing frosts do not occur as early in autumn or as late in spring.

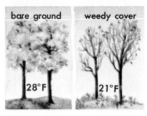

BARE GROUND areas may be warmer on cold nights then weedy areas, because the weeds interfere with the upward radiation of heat from the ground. On frost nights, plants surrounded by bare areas have a greater chance of survival than do those in areas covered by a thick ground cover and leaf litter.

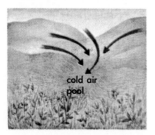

DEPRESSIONS in the surface of the earth can act as cold air traps. On windless nights, cold air flows downhill and, like water, collects in lowland pockets. Cold-sensitive plants may be absent from these low areas, though they may thrive on the nearby, warmer high ground. The effect of frost pockets in vegetation can be seen in slightly rolling terrains especially in sub-tropics.

TREE CANOPIES protect the plants that grow underneath. In cold weather, the canopy reflects heat back to the ground. In summer, the shade prevents the temperature from becoming high. At times only a few degrees of difference in temperature may be recorded, but this may be the critical difference for survival. Humidity is also important.

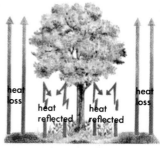

UNDERGROUND WATER may come close to the surface in some areas of deserts and change completely the character of the vegetation compared to the surroundings. These areas are called oases. In the Kofa Mountains of southwestern Arizona, for example, palms grow in a steep, desert canyon where water seeps out of the rocks.

palm tree oasis in desert canyon

PLANTS ALTER HABITATS as they grow. In a field of grain or grass, for example, the temperature, humidity, and wind may vary considerably from the ground to the top of the plants. Insects adapted to particular niches move up or down the plants to remain comfortable as the microenvironment changes.

Height	Wind Vel.	Temp.
24 in.	10 ft/sec	69°F
16	4 ft/sec	70°
10	2 ft/sec	69.8°
4	0	66.2°

GREENHOUSES are useful microhabitats in which temperature, light, and moisture can be controlled. Even within a greenhouse, microclimatic conditions exist. Plants that require full sunlight are hung from the roof; those with intermediate needs are placed on the benches in semishade; those that need almost complete shade are placed under the benches.

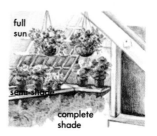

full sun

semi-shade

complete shade

153

INTERACTIONS occur as living things respond to each other and to their environment. Ecologists sometimes describe the complex relationships as (1) commensalism and mutualism, in which the relationships are either beneficial or neutral; and (2) competition, parasitism, and predation, in which they are inhibiting or harmful.

COMPETITION is the principal interaction among plants. Plants of the same species are the most strongly competitive, because they have the same needs and the same structures for obtaining them. They interfere with or prevent each other from getting sunlight, water, and minerals.

Some plants eliminate competitors of their own species by producing growth-inhibiting substances. Roots of the desert Creosote Bush, for example, secrete toxic substances that kill young seedlings that germinate nearby. This results in the natural wide spacing of the bushes, as shown in the illustration below left. Encelia, another desert shrub, and Black Walnuts are other plants that inhibit growth of their own seedlings when nearby.

Plants may also eliminate competition from other species, as shown in the aerial view below right. The patches of gray-green sagebrush are separated from the green grasslands by narrow bands of soil. Leaves of the shrubs give off a gaseous chemical that kills the grass, which is yellowed and dead where it has grown toward the shrub islands.

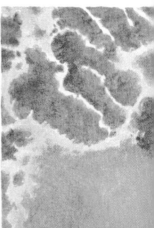

PLANTS ARE USEFUL INDICATORS of atmospheric pollution. In some cases symptoms appearing on crops or on wild plants are the first evidence that pollution is occurring, hence serve as a warning system. Millions of dollars are being lost each year due to damage by atmospheric pollutants to crop and wild plants.

AIR POLLUTION capable of killing plants first became evident years ago with the expansion of industries. Smoke was the first obvious cause.

The airborne toxicants responsible for most plant kills today are ethylene, ozone, aldehydes, fluorides, sulfur and nitrogen dioxide, and several components of smog. Ethylene can damage some plants at concentrations in the air as low as 5 parts per hundred million. Shown here are some vegetables damaged by smog in California. In this condition the vegetables are not salable.

Pinto Bean

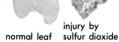

injury by ozone   normal leaf   injury by sulfur dioxide

Celery   Romaine Lettuce

injury by nitrogen dioxide

RADIATION effects on plants range from slight, almost undetectable injuries to abnormal growths, growth stoppage, and even death. To study its effect on a plant community, gamma radiation sources were placed in an oak-pine forest. About six months later, the effects were easily seen as far as 120 feet from the source. Sedges were the most tolerant species, pines the least. Obviously, uncontrolled radioactive pollution can alter plant and animal communities in ways that may be vitally important to man.

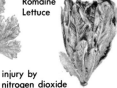

blue   pines, oaks, heaths, sedges—all alive
green   pines killed
orange   pines and oaks killed
yellow   pines, oaks, and heaths killed
gray   all plants dead
red   • source of radiation

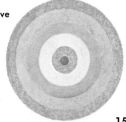

Relative Tolerance of Plants to Radiation

3½ BILLION PEOPLE 1970

6 BILLION PEOPLE 2000

?

MAN'S ECOSYSTEM is dependent upon plants. Plants are the basis of his food and are the links to all energy and material cycles between the earth and the sun.

Man has replaced large forested areas with low-growing seasonal crops, roads, and cities. In so doing, fertile soils have been destroyed and natural drainages altered. Extensive drought areas appear, persist, and increase year after year. Due to increased release of carbon dioxide into the atmosphere, beyond the capacity of green plants to control, a "greenhouse effect" at high altitudes is causing the earth to become warmer. More changes to the environment seem inescapable as man's population continues to increase. We must make more intelligent use of our resources if we are to survive.

Many scientific advances help. Improved varieties of food plants are being produced giving greater crop yields. A cross between wheat and rye, for example, has produced an entirely new species and a superior grain. Improved plant sources of drugs, fibers, and raw materials for industries are being discovered regularly.

Adjustments to changes will always be necessary as more is learned about how to control and to direct the environment. It is essential to keep a huge area of the earth in plants as a basis for the pyramid of life. Increasing numbers of humans will require an even broader plant base for this pyramid.

FOR FURTHER REFERENCE

Fuller, Harry J., and Carothers, Zane B., *The Plant World,* 4th ed., New York, N.Y.: Holt, Rinehart & Winston, 1963.

Milne, Lorus and Margery, *Living Plants of the World,* New York, N.Y.: Random House, 1967.

Northen, Henry T., *Introductory Plant Science,* 3rd ed., New York, N.Y.: Ronald Press, 1968

Raven, Peter H., and Curtis, Helena, *Biology of Plants,* New York, N.Y.: Worth Publishers, 1970

Shuttleworth, Floyd S., and Zim, Herbert S., *Non-Flowering Plants,* New York, N.Y.: Golden Press, 1967

Tortora, Gerard J., Cicero, Donald R., and Parish, Howard I., *Plant Form and Function,* New York, N.Y.: Crowell Collier & Macmillan, 1970

Wilson, Carl L., and Loomis, Walter A., *Botany,* 4th ed., New York, N.Y.: Holt, Rinehart & Winston, 1967

INDEX

157